SPIRITUAL BLESSINGS

C.A. COATES

Printed and published by Bible and Gospel Trust, Chelwood House
Cox Lane, Chessington, Surrey, England KT9 1DN

THE FORGIVENESS OF SINS

I desire to bring before you at this time a very important subject, the Forgiveness of Sins. Some may think it an elementary subject to bring before a company of believers, but I am quite sure it is a subject which many believers have not apprehended in its greatness and blessedness. We too often think of it from the side of man's need only, and by so doing we are apt to lose sight of the greatness and grace of it according to God.

In the first place, then, let us consider

THE PROCLAMATION OF FORGIVENESS.

The Lord Jesus "said unto them, Thus it is written, and thus it behoved Christ to suffer, and to rise from the dead the third day: and that repentance and remission of sins should be preached in His name among all nations, beginning at Jerusalem" (Luke 24: 46, 47). Paul at Antioch says, "Be it known unto you therefore, men and brethren, that through this man is preached unto you the forgiveness of sins: and by Him, all that believe are justified from all things, from which ye could not be justified by the law of Moses" (Acts 13: 38, 39).

The first thing that demands attention as to this blessed proclamation is the fact that it is altogether on God's part. It does not suppose or require the fulfilment of any conditions on the part of man. It rather, indeed, assumes and takes for granted at the outset that nothing attaches to man but SINS. It is the unconditional declaration on God's part of His disposition towards men. On their part they may be ungodly and impenitent, too hardened by familiarity with sin to feel their need, too proud to own it even if they feel it, or too much in love with their sins to wish to part company with them; but all this, sad as it is, does not in any way affect the proclamation of forgiveness, either to change its character or to limit its scope. God would have men to know what He is, and to know that His grace is greater than their sins, and to this end He sends forth this gracious proclamation. It is entirely OF and FROM GOD.

Then it is preached in the name of the Lord Jesus, and through Him. A name sets forth the character, reputation, renown, dignity, and glory of the one to whom it belongs. Now it is in the NAME of the Lord Jesus that forgiveness of sins is proclaimed. What lustre and honour is thus put upon the proclamation! With what exceeding grace and attractiveness is it presented to men! We are not called upon, as it were, to look at the guilty sinner in his fearful need and danger; our eyes are at once directed to a Saviour in whom every perfection is found. Not the leper in his sores, but the mighty and gracious Healer, is before us. In short, we do not find ourselves in the presence of man's need and ruin, but in the presence of God's infinite grace.

Think of this blessed One, in whose name forgiveness of sins is proclaimed; seek to get before your heart something of His greatness and preciousness. He is One who came into this world to bring the full revelation of God into it, and at the same time to present absolute perfection in manhood to the eye of God in the very scene and circumstances where Adam and his children had so thoroughly broken down; He was One able to make atonement, to overcome death, to vanquish Satan, to spoil principalities and powers, and to glorify God as to the whole question of sin; He was One who filled up and presented in His own person every prophetic blessing, whether connected with the Son of David, the Son of Abraham, the Son of man, or the Son of God; He is One who has finished the work God gave Him to do, who has glorified God by bringing every divine attribute into full and eternal display, and who has set the nature of God free to have its own way in blessing, even in a scene where everything had been ruined by sin; He is One now raised by the glory of the Father, and seated in heavenly exaltation at the right hand of the majesty on high. And

IN HIS NAME

forgiveness of sins is preached among all nations, and to every creature under heaven. With what power and preciousness does the proclamation go forth! It goes forth according to all the worthiness, excellence, perfection, grace, and glory of CHRIST, and invested with all the authority and attractiveness of His name. Important addresses to honoured individuals are often inscribed upon costly vellum, and ornamented with every device that art can suggest; but was ever address or proclamation inscribed upon such a scroll as that on which God has inscribed His proclamation of grace to a world of lost and guilty sinners? God has invested that proclamation with all the beauty and glory of Christ, and with the power and preciousness of His sacred NAME. One might say that God has made forgiveness of sins as attractive as possible by setting it forth in the name of the Lord Jesus.

'*Through this man* is preached unto you the forgiveness of sins.' God puts Christ before sinners—the Son of His love, the blessed Victim of Calvary, now the risen and glorified One—and through HIM proclaims forgiveness. On the platform of divine grace—on which God approaches man with this wondrous proclamation—there is but one figure to be seen, and that is CHRIST. It is on the ground of what HE is, and in connection with the worthiness and glory of His Person, that forgiveness of sins is proclaimed. The gospel of God is "concerning His Son Jesus Christ our Lord." Our goodness, repentance, desire to amend, prayers, religious service, or works of any kind, have absolutely nothing to do with it; and, on the other hand, our sins—impiety, self-will, pride, indifference, self-satisfaction, blasphemy, hypocrisy, or whatever other form of wickedness we may have been guilty of in thought, word, or deed—do not in any way detract from the fulness or the freeness of this divine proclamation. The very fact that such a proclamation is addressed to us assumes that we are guilty; it is as such, and in no other way, that it regards us. But it addresses us, not according to our deserts, but according to all the greatness, perfection, and worthiness of the One in whose name it is promulgated.

'Philip went down to the city of Samaria, and preached CHRIST unto them' (Acts 8: 5). CHRIST is the great and blessed theme of the evangelist, and as He is preached faith IN HIM "cometh by hearing." Faith in Christ is not a blind acceptance of certain arbitrary dogmas or the assent of the mind to an orthodox creed. It is the whole-hearted confidence of one who has come to the knowledge of the blessed perfection of Christ as a Saviour. He is everything that He needs to be to fill that place—to be the Mediator of God and men. Nothing can be added to Him. He is everything to God's satisfaction, and He is everything that the heart and conscience of an exercised sinner would like Him to be. He is a suitable, an acceptable, and an attractive Saviour. And He is the only One; He has no rival; it is Christ or nothing. "Through this man is preached unto you the forgiveness of sins" (Acts 13: 38).

This proclamation is universal in its scope; it is to go forth "among all nations." It is also unlimited in its application to the individual. God does not offer a partial discharge. He does not say 'sins that are repented of,' nor 'sins that are confessed,' nor 'sins up to the time of believing,' but simply "forgiveness of sins." The whole question of sins is looked at as one thing, and when you get the forgiveness of sins you get it for ever. If it were otherwise there could never be any certainty about the matter. How could the believer ever be sure that he had not overlooked some of his sins? Or if every fresh sin committed raised again the whole question of the believer's forgiveness and justification, it would be quite impossible for any to have the quiet confidence of peace with God or the certainty of forgiveness, which is the very groundwork in the soul of all happy relationship with God. I purpose later on to say a little about sins committed after conversion, both as to how they affect the believer's heart and conscience, and as to how they are dealt with. But for the present I desire to press the importance of seeing that the forgiveness of sins, which clears the believer of all imputation in the sight of a holy God, is something which is unchanging and eternal. There is no thought in Scripture of a believer having it today and not having it tomorrow.

But before saying more as to this I should like to bring under your notice several Scriptures with reference to

THE ASSURANCE OF FORGIVENESS:

Acts 10: 43; 1 John 2: 12; Col. 1: 14. Doubts and misgivings on the subject of forgiveness arise from the fact that anxious souls are slow to believe that the proclamation is one of absolute grace, that it is presented to them in the name of the Lord Jesus, and that it is entirely "for His name's sake." They look upon it as a sort of conditional offer on God's part to obtain the benefit of which there must be the fulfilment of certain conditions on their part; and as they cannot be quite sure that they have fulfilled the conditions, they are in a state of uncertainty on the whole matter. They do not know whether they have repented enough, or whether they have faith enough, or whether they have the right kind of faith. These difficulties, and many others which trouble anxious souls, only show how little they have apprehended the grace of God. We are so slow to take in the blessed thought that God is acting *from Himself* and according to the worthiness of CHRIST, and that there is no question of any conditions to be fulfilled on our side. The whole thing is complete on God's side, and is not in any way conditional on our repentance or faith; it is God approaching man in all the fulness of His grace, and declaring Himself to be a Saviour-God.

I find nothing in myself that I can trust in the smallest degree, but I can trust the grace in which God has set Himself forth in Christ. It is GOD who has spoken to me of forgiveness of sins, and who has set this great blessing before me in the name of the Lord Jesus and through Him. I gladly receive this wondrous grace, for it brings me what I need, and at the same time bows my heart in adoration before the unexpected and unmerited favour of God. I believe on God as the Source of the whole blessing, and as the One who has provided it altogether from His own side; and I believe on the Lord Jesus as the Mediator of that grace, as the One who has opened up a righteous channel for it, and in whose name it is proclaimed. And the Word of God declares that "through His name whosoever believeth in Him shall receive remission of sins" (Acts 10: 43). There is no question or peradventure about it. The blessing is certain to "whosoever believeth in Him."

But the question will arise in some hearts, "Is it not possible to believe in a way that leaves a man a mere professor? We read that "Simon himself believed also" (Acts 8: 13), and he turned out to be one that had "neither part nor lot in this matter." It is written that "the devils also believe, and tremble"

(James 2: 19). How, then, can one be sure that his faith is such as will secure the blessing of God?

I must again point out that the thought which lies behind this question is that *faith* is a condition which has to be fulfilled on our part before the grace of God is available for us. That is, the soul has the idea that the grace of God is conditional upon faith, but conditional grace is not really grace at all. The gospel of the grace of God is the proclamation of the blessed fact that God is coming out in absolute grace on the ground of the death of Christ, and according to all the perfections of Christ, and is proclaiming forgiveness of sins to a world of sinners. When this gospel is believed it brings the knowledge of God in all the blessedness of His unconditional grace into the heart of the sinner. But the sinner's faith adds nothing to the gospel any more than the windows of our houses add to the light of the sun. The sun shines for everybody; my window lets the light into my room so that I enjoy it and am warmed by it. In like manner the sun of divine grace is shining for everybody; faith is the window which lets the light and warmth of it into the soul of a sinner. If you appreciate that grace and rejoice in it as the only thing that could possibly meet the need of your soul, you need have no question as to the nature of your faith. You may be sure that Simon Magus had no appreciation of the grace of God. He was intellectually convinced, it may be, by the miracles done by Philip; the new religion had credentials that could not be disputed, and, moreover, it was for the moment the popular thing. By the sheer force of evidences and circumstances, he accepted and professed it, but there is nothing to show that he had the smallest real appreciation of the grace which Philip preached as he proclaimed Christ in the city. The devils may believe that there is one God, and tremble as they believe, but you may be sure they have no appreciation whatever of divine grace.

A man may "say" he has faith; he may "say" that he believes in the grace of God; but if his heart is not cheered and gladdened by it, it is evident that it is nothing to him. The knowledge of grace subdues a man to God; it breaks the power of sin, and it brings heavenly gladness into the heart. In short, it brings the knowledge of God into the heart of man. The sinner who believes has the light of what God is in his heart. He only thinks of himself as a corrupt and hell-deserving sinner, but he knows what God is in absolute and unconditional grace for sinners; he knows something of the preciousness and worthiness of Christ. It is not that he believes in his own faith—anyone who did so would be on very dangerous ground—he believes God's proclamation of grace, and rejoices in that grace because it not only meets his need, but makes God known to him so that he can "joy in God."

Those who have misgivings about their faith are not generally those who despise the grace of God. It is more often those who realise something of the value of that grace, and feel they must perish without it, that are concerned lest they should not have it for themselves. Let me say to such that that grace has already, to some extent at any rate, established itself in your heart. The window may be small, and the rays of light are only few that have yet entered, but the light has begun to shine even in your soul. What you need is to turn away from yourself—your feelings and your faith—to the blessed God of all grace. He is what He is, whether you believe it or not; believing it brings the knowledge and gladness of it into your heart.

It is "for His name's sake" that the believer's sins are forgiven. It is because of what Christ is, and according to the value of His atoning death, that God can say to every believer on His blessed name, "your sins are forgiven." And believers can say without question or doubt, 'in whom *we have* redemption through His blood, even the forgiveness of sins' (Col. 1: 14).

What many souls need, in order to establish them in assurance, is to see

THE RIGHTEOUS GROUND OF FORGIVENESS

as we have it clearly and fully presented in the Word of God. I desire to direct your attention in particular to Hebrews 10, where we learn that forgiveness is founded upon a sacrifice in which God has been glorified in righteousness. Let us then briefly consider what is presented to us in the first eighteen verses of this chapter.

A careful reader cannot fail to notice that two things are prominent in these verses: first, the accomplishment of the will of God; and second, the securing a purged and perfected conscience for those who approach God. The second is really included in the first, for the will or pleasure of God may be briefly summed up in this, that He would make Himself known, and that He would have a people free in conscience and happy in heart to approach Him according to the revelation of Himself. The first covenant, and all that was connected with it, entirely failed to accomplish either of these two things. God found fault with the first covenant, as we are told in Hebrews 8, because it failed to make Him known in the hearts of His people; and the law, with the whole system of sacrifices connected with it, is taken away in Hebrews 10, because it was so entirely powerless to give a purged conscience to those who approached God.

But now in connection with Christ we get all the grace of the new covenant, God revealed in supreme and blessed grace on the one hand, and on the other His people purged and perfected in their consciences, so that they may be able to "draw near with a true heart." Consequent upon the death of Christ two things are made good: believers are (1) "sanctified" and (2) "perfected for ever" (verses 10, 14). "Then said He, Lo, I come to do Thy will, O God… By the which will we are sanctified, through the offering of the body of Jesus Christ once." Believers are sanctified, or set apart, according to the pleasure of God. It is His pleasure to have a people whom He can regard according to His own estimate of the value of the death of Christ; it is His pleasure to have a people entirely divested of every trace of unsuitability to Himself; and this not by a progressive work carried on in them, but by the infinite efficacy of the "offering of the body of Jesus Christ."

As to what the believer is in himself, Hebrews 10 supposes that he is nothing but a heap of sins. Morally my whole history is covered by that one word SINS. As a child of fallen Adam, nothing could come out of me but sins, the sad evidence of my corruption and irretrievable ruin. But in the "offering of the body of Jesus Christ" God has been glorified in the execution of a righteous sentence upon me and my sins. Christ has gone into death vicariously, and in His death there has been such a judgment of sin and sins that in the eyes of God not a stain of guilt, not a spot of contamination, remains upon His people. They are set apart in the will of God, and according to His pleasure, from everything that they were naturally and from everything that attached to them as Adam's children in this world. Such is the efficacy and such is the result of the death of Christ looked at from God's side. It has secured for Him a sanctified people suited to Himself.

But, on the other hand, this has to be made known and to be made good in the consciences of believers, or they would have no liberty to approach God. Hence we read, "For by one offering He hath perfected for ever them that are sanctified." If we compare this statement with chapter 9: 9, we shall see that the perfection here referred to is perfection "pertaining to the conscience." It is not by any means that the believer is brought into a state of perfection as to his actual condition in this world; we shall only attain perfection in *condition* when we are conformed to the image of God's Son in glory, but perfection in *conscience* we not only *may* know now, but if we have it not we must be more or less in legal darkness and in ignorance of the true grace of God.

The believer is in his conscience with God, not as identified with his sins and all the imperfection that attached to him as a man in this world, but as identified with the value of the "one offering" of Christ. He knows the efficacy of that offering and rejoices in it as that by which his sins have been completely and eternally purged. It is not that he thinks lightly of his sins, but he has come to know and appreciate the value of the death of Christ. That death has cleared everything away in the estimation of God, so that He can have His people before Him in the beauty of divine sanctification, and it has cleared everything away in the estimation of the believer's conscience, enlightened by grace, so that every question of sins is settled; he is as to this matter "perfected." And inasmuch as the ground of this perfection is the unalterable value of the death of Christ, he is "perfected for ever." The believer's place with God according to divine grace is not changeable; he is not sometimes on the ground of Christ's death and sometimes on the ground of his own good behaviour. The value of the "one offering" does not fluctuate with his changing moods and feelings, nor with the ebbings and flowings of his joy. It abides as the only and the unchanging ground on which God can have a people for Himself. The believer who apprehends this is on solid ground; he is acquainted with the grace of God, and he knows the secure basis on which all the activities of that grace are based; he is perfected in perpetuity.

There is another thing in the chapter before us which connects itself with all this in a very blessed way. I refer to verse 16: "I will put My laws into their hearts, and in their minds will I write them; and their sins and iniquities will I remember no more." Here we see the effect of grace being known in the hearts of men. It becomes a pleasure to them to be controlled by the will of God, for the things which are on a man's heart and mind are things which give him pleasure: and along with this they have the blessed consciousness that the question of their sins has been entirely and eternally disposed of. The great thought of God is to have His people near Himself, with not a single outstanding question between Himself and them, and this in order that they may find their undistracted delight in Him and in being controlled by His pleasure. God would have His people conscious that there is nothing between Himself and them; He would have them conscious that they are a forgiven people, that thus they may realise the "blessedness" which David describes in Psalm 32: "Blessed is he whose transgression is forgiven, whose sin is covered. Blessed is the man unto whom the Lord imputeth not iniquity, and in whose spirit there is no guile." This is

THE JOY OF FORGIVENESS,

the happy portion of a people "illuminated" (Heb. 10: 32) by divine grace.

But some man will say, 'If the whole question of the believer's sins is thus disposed of he may live as he likes, and, no matter how badly he behaves, he is always forgiven.' In answer to this often-raised objection, I repeat what I have already said, that the effect of the grace of God being known in the soul is to thoroughly subdue a man in the presence of God. The knowledge of forgiveness *never* has the effect of making a man careless about sin. 'There is forgiveness with Thee, *that Thou mayest be feared*' (Psalm 130: 4). The knowledge of grace establishes the fear of God in the heart of everyone who has it in truth. The *forgiven* man is a *godly* man. In Psalm 32, after describing the blessedness of the forgiven man, David goes on to say, 'For this shall every one that is GODLY pray unto Thee in a time when Thou mayest be found.' And the New Testament puts things in exactly the same order, for we read that 'the grace of God that bringeth salvation hath appeared to all men, teaching us, that, denying ungodliness and worldly lusts, we should live soberly, righteously, and GODLY, in this present world' (Titus 2: 11, 12). It is the believer's joy, as we have already seen, to be controlled by the will of God.

On the other hand, it is never stated in Scripture that the believer has no sin in him, or that he is beyond the reach of temptation or the danger of being overtaken in a fault. He is warned, if he thinks that he stands secure, to take heed lest he fall; he is warned against the deceitfulness of sin and the wiles of the devil; he is solemnly exhorted not to love the world, and to abstain from fleshly lusts, which war against the soul. He has need to be in constant dependence, and to watch and pray that he may not enter into temptation. And practically it is true, as James says, that 'in many things we all offend.' But the more we know of the blessedness of forgiveness, the more sensitive we shall be to any shade that comes upon it. If we have tasted the deep joy of being in the presence of God, with the consciousness of His infinite grace and the knowledge that that grace has removed in righteousness everything that was between Himself and us, we shall not be in any way disposed to tolerate or allow the activity of sin.

We shall dread sin; we shall avoid it; we shall flee from it; we shall pray continually, "lead us not into temptation, but deliver us from evil."

And yet God would not have us to lose the sense of His grace even when, through lack of dependence or purpose of heart, we have sinned. His grace has anticipated the possibility of our doing so, and has made provision for such a case: "if any man sin, we have an advocate with the Father, Jesus Christ the righteous" (1 John 2: 1). And as to our side it is written that, "if we confess our sins, He is faithful and just to forgive us our sins, and to cleanse us from all unrighteousness" (1 John 1: 9). The very fact that we have sinned is the proof that in some degree we have departed from the sense of God's wondrous grace. No one could sin if his heart was in the consciousness of the grace of God, and restoration is the return of our souls to a sense of grace.

How far is the light and joy of divine favour the sunshine and life of our hearts? In proportion as it is so we shall be quick to feel the presence of a shade or a cloud. We shall make haste to confess our sins, not merely to get them off our minds or consciences, but to get near to God about the things which have for the moment intercepted the "blessedness" of our joy in His grace.

In conclusion, I should like to say a few words about

THE EFFECT OF FORGIVENESS

in its practical bearing on the believer's state. In the first place, when forgiveness is consciously known as we have it presented in Scripture the soul is entirely on the ground of what CHRIST is. Indeed, it is IN HIM that we have it, as Ephesians 1: 7 and Colossians 1: 14 state so plainly: "in whom we have redemption through His blood, the forgiveness of sins." In the apprehension of this there is entire deliverance from the power of the enemy. Satan may challenge *my* clearance and *my* acceptance, he may raise all kinds of questions about what *I* am and what *I* have done, but he can raise no question as to the worthiness or acceptance of CHRIST. The forgiven man is on an altogether new ground with God; he is on the ground of grace—grace which is set forth in CHRIST. The apprehension of this is redemption, and it puts the soul beyond the reach of the oppression and harassing of the enemy.

This leaves the believer free in his spirit to approach God. God has brought us out of everything that attached to us in our responsibility as children of Adam, that we might be free to approach Him on another ground altogether; He has forgiven us all trespasses, that we might be free to apprehend His pleasure concerning us, that we might know what it is to be quickened together with Christ (Col. 2: 13). There is an entire settlement of every question connected with our responsible history, so that we may approach God as those whose hearts and consciences are free to enter into a circle where there is nothing but the perfection of Christ. If we have learned that God has approached us in His wondrous grace according to the preciousness and perfection of Christ—if God has dealt with us, not according to what we are, but according to what CHRIST is—the suited response to that grace is that we approach Him as those who are in conscious identification with the blessedness and perfection of Christ. This puts us on priestly ground with God; it is the suited state for the sanctuary; we begin to apprehend that God has *brought us out* that He might *bring us in*. He would have us in His own place, where everything is according to His own thoughts and according to the perfection of Christ. I do not think that anyone who had the consciousness of forgiveness according to God would care to stop short of this. Hence the writer of the epistle immediately follows up what he had been saying in Hebrews 10 about forgiveness of sins by the words, "Having therefore, brethren, boldness to enter into the holiest by the blood of Jesus, by a new and living way, which He hath consecrated for us, through the veil, that is to say, His flesh; and having an High Priest over the house of God; let us draw near with a true heart, in full assurance of faith, having our hearts sprinkled from an evil conscience, and our bodies washed with pure water."

Here we get one of the greatest Christian privileges—a privilege God would have to be realised in His assembly now: that of approach to Himself in His own circle. Great as this privilege is—and, alas! so feebly entered into by any of us, if one may speak for all—it is, notwithstanding, the great present end, with a view to which God makes known the forgiveness of sins. And I think I may venture to say again that if we really apprehend forgiveness of sins from God's side in all its grace and preciousness, we shall not care to stop short of this great privilege. The effect of forgiveness being consciously known is that we are in the divine peace of redemption on the one hand, and on the other we are greatly attracted by the blessed privilege of approach to God. If these two things are not true of us, it is a question whether we have not been content to apprehend forgiveness from the side of our need, rather than from the side of the divine greatness in which it is presented from God in the gospel of His grace.

JUSTIFICATION

Solid peace must be based upon the knowledge of God as the Justifier. Neither intensity of conviction, nor depth of repentance, nor striking experience, nor religious fervour, nor earnest service can give *peace with God*. There must be the knowledge of God as the Justifier, that is, in the blessed character of grace in which He reveals Himself in the gospel.

But to appreciate what God is as the Justifier we need to know that He has searched us and known us, that He understands our thought afar off, is acquainted with all our ways, and that there is not a word in our tongue that He does not know altogether. (See Psalm 139.) In short, we need to know

OUR NEED OF JUSTIFICATION.

It is a very solemn thing for any of us to face the fact that we have passed under the searching eye of God, and that our every thought is exposed before Him. I suppose we have all, like the psalmist, wished to evade the searchings of God. "Whither shall I go from Thy spirit? or whither shall I flee from Thy presence? If I ascend up into heaven, Thou art there: if I make my bed in hell, behold, Thou art there. If I take the wings of the morning, and dwell in the uttermost parts of the sea; even there shall Thy hand lead me, and Thy right hand shall hold me. If I say, Surely the darkness shall cover me; even the night shall be light about me. Yea, the darkness hideth not from Thee: but the night shineth as the day: the darkness and the light are both alike to Thee" (Psalm 139: 7–12).

A natural man cannot bear the thought of being searched by God; he cannot bear to think of being found out in his true character. But to a truly exercised soul it is a positive comfort to be assured that God knows everything about us; He knows the very worst about us that can ever be discovered. If God has thoughts of blessing concerning us, He has formed those thoughts notwithstanding His perfect knowledge of what we are. He has searched out all that we are, and in spite of all, He has thoughts of blessing concerning us. There is, therefore, no fear of anything coming to light that might cause Him to change or reverse His thoughts of blessing.

That God knows our state thoroughly we may discover by reading Romans 3. Take the following verses, for example:—

‘we have before proved both Jews and Gentiles, that they are ALL UNDER SIN: as it is written, There is none righteous, no, not one: there is none that understandeth, there is none that seeketh after God. They are all gone out of the way, they are together become unprofitable; there is none that doeth good, no, not one… what things soever the law saith, it saith to them who are under the law; that every mouth may be stopped, and ALL THE WORLD MAY BECOME SUBJECT TO THE JUDGMENT OF GOD [note]. Therefore by the deeds of the law there shall no flesh be justified in His sight: for by the law is the knowledge of sin… there is no difference: for ALL HAVE SINNED, AND COME SHORT OF THE GLORY OF GOD’ (Rom. 3: 9–23).

These are sweeping and comprehensive statements. They are too plain to be misunderstood; and it is impossible for any sober-minded person to regard them with levity or indifference. They do not assert that Adam’s children are all alike as to *sinful actions*, but they do declare that all are alike “under sin,” “subject to the judgment of God,” and “come short of the glory of God.” The root-principle from which every sinful action proceeds is the same in every man, woman, and child of Adam’s race. It would be difficult to find two lives that were exactly alike outwardly, but when we pass beneath the surface and consider man's state before God, we find "there is no difference." This being the case, JUSTIFICATION is an absolute necessity for us if we are to be in the way of blessing at all.

Having realised this, we are prepared to learn that

THE SOURCE OF JUSTIFICATION

must be entirely outside man, and altogether of divine grace. It is very striking that in the Psalm already referred to (139), after the full exposure of man's thoughts and ways, the psalmist turns to God and says, 'How precious also are *Thy thoughts* unto me, O God! how great is the sum of them! If I should count them, they are more in number than the sand' (verses 17, 18).

All blessing is the outcome of *the thoughts of God*, and those thoughts are "to us-ward" (Psalm 40: 5); they are thoughts of blessing *for man*. In spite of what man is, it is the thought of God to bless him. The gospel is the revelation of the thoughts of God, and it presents God to us as the Justifier; it is the thought of God to have men justified. So we read, "being justified freely by His grace"; and again, "that He might be just, and the justifier of him which believeth in Jesus"; and again, "it is one God, which shall justify the circumcision by faith, and uncircumcision through faith"; and again, God is spoken of as "Him that justifieth the ungodly" (Rom. 3: 24, 26, 30; 4: 5).

But it may be well, before proceeding farther, to read two or three Scriptures which will give us some idea of

WHAT IT IS TO BE JUSTIFIED.

"In those days, and in that time, saith the Lord, the iniquity of Israel shall be sought for, and there shall be none; and the sins of Judah, and they shall not be found: for I will pardon them whom I reserve" (Jer. 50: 20). "He hath blessed; and I cannot reverse it. He hath not beheld iniquity in Jacob, neither hath He seen perverseness in Israel" (Num. 23: 20, 21). "Blessed are they whose iniquities are forgiven, and whose sins are covered. Blessed is the man to whom the Lord will not impute sin" (Rom. 4: 7, 8).

These Scriptures bring very clearly before us the fact that it is God's mind to justify sinners, that is, to put away their iniquity and sins so as to clear them of all imputation, that He may be able to regard them according to His own thoughts of blessing for them. The more this grace is considered and apprehended, the more wonderful and attractive does it appear to the heart of an exercised sinner. Many would deny this grace, or, at any rate, rob our hearts of all enjoyment of it, by saying that it is impossible to *know* that our sins are forgiven, or to be *sure* that we are justified. But Scripture speaks distinctly of the "blessedness" of the justified man. There is not much blessedness in uncertainty, not much happiness in the heart of an exercised man who does not know whether he is justified or not. David, at any rate, was in no uncertainty when he described "the blessedness of the man, unto whom God imputeth righteousness without works," for he said plainly, 'Thou forgavest the iniquity of MY SIN' (Psalm 32: 5).

The believer's iniquities are forgiven, and his sins are covered. This is the unvarying testimony of the Holy Ghost. (See Acts 10: 43; 13: 38, 39; 1 Cor. 15: 3; Gal. 1: 4; Eph. 1: 7; 4: 32; Col. 1: 14; 2: 13; Heb. 10: 12–18; 1 Peter 2: 24; 1 John 2: 12; Rev. 1: 5.)

Then, further, the justified man is one "to whom the Lord will not impute sin." It is a settled thing in the mind of God, the outcome of His own grace on the righteous ground of the death of Christ, that He will not put sin to the account of the believer. "He hath not beheld iniquity in Jacob, neither hath He seen perverseness in Israel." The believer is accounted by God to be clear of iniquity, sin, imperfection, inconsistency, and of all the unsuitability to God which attaches to him as a sinner in this world.

But the consideration of this at once awakens the question, How can this be accomplished in righteousness; that is, in consistency with what God is and with all His attributes? for we read in Scripture that He "will by no means clear the guilty" (Exod. 34: 7). The nature and attributes of God make it imperative that holy judgment should come upon sin, and yet it is the thought of His grace to justify the ungodly. Here we are confronted with a problem which only divine wisdom and love could solve, a problem which has found its solution, to God's eternal praise and glory, in *the death of Christ*, which is

THE RIGHTEOUS GROUND OF JUSTIFICATION.

If we are "justified freely by His grace," it is "through the redemption that is in Christ Jesus." The extreme penalty has passed upon all alike. "The wages of sin is death." "And so death passed upon all men, for that all have sinned" (Rom. 6: 23; 5: 12). The righteousness of God must be against sin, but in the death of Christ we see that righteousness declared in such a way that it becomes the foundation of blessing. God has expressed His judgment of sin in the fullest way without touching a hair of the sinner's head. Nothing could show God's hatred of sin so much as the fact that Christ has died to bear its judgment, while the fact that He has died has established the righteousness of God in relation to all His actings of grace. The one who was chief of sinners may go into glory on the ground of that death; forgiveness of sins may be proclaimed to the guilty and perishing millions of Adam's race; and not even Satan can say that God is *unrighteous* in His ways of grace.

We can see God's way of dealing with sin in the death of Christ. We see all that is due to God in respect of sin maintained in that death; in a word, we see His righteousness there. But it is all in our favour. We can fall in with God's righteousness, with God's way of dealing with sin, and find that it secures our blessing for ever. On the ground of the death of Christ, God is as righteous in justifying the ungodly sinner who believes in Jesus as He will be righteous in condemning everyone who has not "faith in His blood." We must learn God's righteousness either in grace or in judgment. The believer learns it in the death of Christ; the unbeliever will learn it at the great white throne. Apart from the precious blood of Christ, the whole weight of God's righteousness must be against us. Thank God, that blood is available for us; we may by faith come under its cleansing efficacy and sheltering power; and then "the righteousness of God, which is by faith of Jesus Christ" is upon us, making our blessing eternally sure.

We are justified in virtue of a work of atonement in which God has been glorified in righteousness as to the whole question of sin. The result of God searching man's thoughts is that all the world is found to be subject to His holy judgment. But in wondrous and blessed contrast to this we see the manifestation of God's thoughts of blessing in the fact that Christ has in love become subject to the judgment which lay upon man. In His death the righteousness of God is fully set forth, for therein sin has been judged in the most absolute way. But at the same time the way in which this judgment of sin has come about gives expression to the infinite love of God, for the judgment has been borne by One who came into it as sent and moved by divine love.

At the cross we see Christ in the place and under the judgment of the guilty sinner. The "guilty" has not been "cleared"; on the contrary, judgment has come upon him to the uttermost, but in the person of One who has borne that judgment in love. Nothing attaches to man as a child of Adam but SINS, and he justly lies under the condemnation of DEATH. But God has been so glorified in the death of Christ that His righteousness is '*unto all*.' That is, it is presented in the gospel to every creature under heaven as the only way and ground of blessing for sinners. God is approaching men in boundless grace according to the value of the death of Christ. He is not now in the attitude of a Judge, but a Justifier, and the death of Christ enables Him to be righteously in this attitude. He can approach men according to His own appreciation of the death of Christ, and according to all its meaning and value as known by Him. God is free to give effect to His own thoughts of blessing, and to declare Himself a Justifier and a Saviour-God. He is One "that justifieth the ungodly." And when a sinner believes the testimony of God's grace he is justified. He has faith in the blood of Christ, and God regards him as being under cover of the death of Christ. If God regards a man according to the efficacy of the death of Christ, how much of his ungodliness and guilt is left? Absolutely none! His state and all the guilt that attached to it have received their just condemnation in that wondrous death. The ungodly man who believes God is justified because God can regard him as being under cover of Christ's death, as being entirely removed in that death, with all the iniquity that attached to him. It is a perfect and blessed clearance, that leaves no disturbing element behind.

Having thus seen something of what justification is, we may now briefly consider

THE PRINCIPLE ON WHICH ALONE
WE MAY BE JUSTIFIED.

The clear and simple statements of Romans 4 leave no uncertainty as to this. But, in the first place, we are warned against five roads which *do not lead to justification*.

1. This great blessing comes not by *natural descent*. It was not enough for the Jew to be descended from Abraham. He must needs walk in the steps of *Abraham's faith*. Otherwise he would find himself among those "children of the kingdom" who "shall be cast out into outer darkness" (Matt. 8: 12). See Rom. 4: 11–18. It is a great privilege to be a child of believing parents, but this *will not justify*.

2. Nor can we be justified *by the law*. For, if so, *faith* would be "made void, and the promise made of none effect" (Rom. 4: 14). The law has the opposite effect to justifying—it "worketh wrath" (4: 15)—and in Romans 3: 20 we are plainly told that 'by the deeds of the law there shall no flesh be justified in His sight: for by the law is *the knowledge of sin*.' In another part of Scripture we read that 'as many as are of the works of the law, are *under the curse*,' and "that no man is justified by the law in the sight of God, it is evident: for, The just shall live by faith. And the law is not of faith: but, The man that doeth them shall live in them" (Gal. 3: 10–12).

3. It is equally impossible to be justified by *works of any kind*. Thus boasting is excluded, and all the pretensions of man set aside. (See Rom. 3: 27; 4: 2–4.) It is the faith of 'him that *worketh not*' that is counted to him for righteousness. God imputes to the believer 'righteousness *without works*' (Rom. 4: 5, 6).

4. Nor have *ordinances* any part in this matter of justification. It was "Not in circumcision, but in uncircumcision," that "faith was reckoned to Abraham for righteousness" (Rom. 4: 9–11). Neither baptism nor the Lord's supper confers any saving grace or benefit. To suppose that they do is an awful perversion of those sacred institutions, and a soul-destroying delusion.

5. Finally, it might be urged that, at any rate, a man must be godly and pious before God would justify

him. But the Scripture before us will not allow that this is the case. It is expressly said that God 'justifieth the UNGODLY' (Rom. 4: 5). So that it is neither by natural descent, nor of the law, nor by works, nor through ordinances, nor because of our piety, that we are justified. "Therefore we conclude that a man is

JUSTIFIED BY FAITH,"

without cause or merit in himself of any kind (Rom. 3: 28). And three statements in Romans 4 will, I trust, make clear to us the nature of the faith that justifies:—

1. "Abraham believed God, and it was counted unto him for righteousness" (verse 3).

2. "But to him that worketh not, but believeth on Him that justifieth the ungodly, his faith is counted for righteousness" (verse 5).

3. "Now it was not written for his sake alone, that it was imputed" (or counted) "to him: but for us also, to whom it shall be imputed" (or counted), "if we believe on Him that raised up Jesus our Lord from the dead; who was delivered for our offences, and was raised again for our justification" (verses 23–25).

It is well that we should ponder the deeply instructive illustration of faith which is here presented so prominently. Abraham was childless, and, according to nature, beyond the possibility of having seed, when God "brought him forth abroad, and said, Look now toward heaven, and tell the stars, if thou be able to number them: and He said unto him, So shall thy seed be" (Gen. 15: 5). If Abraham had thought of himself, he would have said, 'This is impossible.' But his eye was altogether turned from himself TO GOD. There are no difficulties or impossibilities with GOD, and "Abraham believed GOD." The thing promised was wholly outside the range of sight, reason, and experience. In fact, it was outside the course of nature altogether, and could only be brought about in the power of *resurrection*. The God in whom he believed was the "God who quickeneth the dead, and calleth those things which be not as though they were."

Now the justification of an ungodly man is as great an impossibility, if you leave God out, as the birth of Isaac or the resurrection of a dead man. If we ask in the sphere of reason and nature, 'Can a dead man be raised?' the answer would be 'Impossible!' In the same sphere it is just as impossible for an ungodly man to be justified. But with God nothing is impossible, and He *has* raised One from the dead, and He *does* justify the ungodly sinner who believes on Him as the One who has done this. What a comfort and joy to the heart of a convicted sinner to know that God "justifieth the ungodly"! Do you believe on Him in this character? If so, your "faith is counted for righteousness." Truly this makes nothing of us, but it makes much of God and of His wondrous grace, by which we are justified freely.

Mark this well, that righteousness shall be imputed to us "if we believe on Him that raised up Jesus our Lord from the dead; who was delivered for our offences, and was raised again for our justification." This brings us to the consideration of

THE MEASURE AND CHARACTER OF JUSTIFICATION,

as set forth in Christ risen. The righteousness which God imputes to the believer is set forth in Jesus our Lord. He is for ever beyond the range of sin, law, judgment, and death, in absolute and eternal suitability to God, and to that new world which He has entered as raised from the dead. And HE IS THE RIGHTEOUSNESS OF EVERY BELIEVER. Our justification is set forth in CHRIST. Hence we are 'justified *by faith*.' If we were justified in ourselves there would be no need for faith; it is because we are justified in Another that faith comes in. "*By Him,* all that believe are justified from all things" (Acts 13: 39).

If we look at ourselves, we see much that will not do for God; but if we look at our risen Saviour, we see nothing but perfect and eternal suitability to God. And all that is set forth in HIM is put to the account of the believer. We have been divested by His death of every spot and stain of sin, and now we see in HIM the perfection of the righteousness with which we are invested in the eyes of God. HE is our righteousness, and as we apprehend and appropriate Him thus we are "justified by faith."

In the death of Christ we see the end of one order of things, and in His resurrection we see the beginning of another. Morally there was nothing connected with *us* but "offences," and Christ went into death to remove all that by bearing its judgment, that thus He might bring to an end before God an order of things in which nothing but iniquity, transgression, and sin were found. But in His resurrection we see MAN introduced to an entirely new position, placed, as we have said, beyond death and judgment, and outside the range of sin and the law, in perfect and eternal suitability to the pleasure of God. That this is absolutely true of Christ no believer would think for a moment of doubting. But it is an immense thing to see that He has been raised again with a view to God's thoughts concerning *us*—He has been raised "for our justification." And if we would learn the character of the righteousness which is imputed to us by God, we must look at that risen One. We are identified before God—that is, in the mind of God—with all the perfection of Christ. Christ is made unto us righteousness.

Now what is the effect of the soul's apprehension of this by faith? Cloudless and everlasting peace. Every question is settled. Satan cannot touch our Lord Jesus Christ. He can never bring a spot or a cloud on the acceptance of that blessed One. And HE is our righteousness. We have come into the knowledge of what God Himself has effected that He might carry out His own thoughts of blessing towards us. He has taken everything into account, and has cleared away in holy judgment all that we were in our sins that He might impute righteousness to us. And the measure and character of that righteousness is set forth in Christ risen.

The soul that is thoroughly established thus in the grace of God is prepared to go further, and to learn something of what is meant by

"JUSTIFICATION OF LIFE."

"Therefore, as by the offence of one judgment came upon all men to condemnation; even so by the righteousness of One the free gift came upon all men unto justification of life. For as by one man's disobedience many were made sinners, so by the obedience of One shall many be made righteous" (Rom. 5: 18, 19). The Holy Ghost is here contrasting Adam and Christ as heads of races. According to nature we have derived character and constitution from Adam, but according to grace we derive a new moral character and constitution from Christ. Adam committed "one offence," and its effect has extended to all his race "to condemnation," for "by one man sin entered into the world, and death by sin; and so death passed upon all men, for that all have sinned" (verse 12). We have derived by natural descent a constitution *of sin* from Adam. By the disobedience of one man the many connected with him have been constituted sinners. But as believers we derive, in a spiritual way, a new moral constitution from Christ. The idea may be a little difficult to grasp for any who have not considered it, but it is in itself very simple and blessed, and will amply repay any prayerful meditation that may be given to it.

Christ has accomplished righteousness, and His "one righteousness" is "towards all men for justification of life." The death of Christ, regarded from this point of view, has a very wide scope; it is "towards all men." It is on God's part the great setting forth to men of righteousness, of the true desert of sin, and of the holy judgment of God, and this withal in absolute grace. God would have men to learn righteousness in the death of Christ—that is, in the way of unmingled grace—that they may derive a new moral constitution from Christ, and have "justification of life." By a new moral constitution I mean that the believer gets a true apprehension in his soul of righteousness according to God. The death of Christ sets forth that judgment must come upon all that we are as in the flesh, and the believer accepts this; yea, he rejoices in the fact that judgment has come upon him in the way of grace in the death of Christ. This is certainly a feature which could by no means be found in a natural man. All the lust, pride, and self-importance of man rebels against such a thought, but the believer, through grace, rejoices in it. He has an entirely new estimate of things—a divine estimate of sin and of righteousness. He recognises that nothing attached to him as a man in the flesh but sin, and he rejoices to know that it has all been judged in the death of Christ. And, on the other hand, he loves to trace the moral beauty, the excellence, the perfection, of CHRIST as that alone which could be acceptable to God or appreciated by Him. He accepts the judgment which he once refused, and that which was once worthless in his eyes is now of inestimable value. He is thus "constituted righteous" as deriving morally from Christ. In short, he has acquired a new moral constitution by learning righteousness and love in the death of Christ, and by coming into the presence of all that grace and moral perfection which is set forth in the Lord Jesus Christ, all of which he enters into in the power of the Holy Ghost given to him to this end.

Hence the believer is not only *accounted* righteous, as we have seen before, but he is *constituted* righteous—he comes into "justification of life." And the practical outcome of this is that he walks in self-judgment, and is taught by the grace of God to live "soberly, righteously, and godly, in this present world" (Titus 2: 12). He fulfils the righteous requirement of the law, and brings forth the fruit of the Spirit—"love, joy, peace, longsuffering, gentleness, goodness, faith, meekness, temperance." It is well said that "against such there is no law" (Gal. 5: 22, 23). Such a one has "justification of life."

In conclusion, I would like to refer briefly to a Scripture which speaks of our being

JUSTIFIED BY WORKS:

James 2: 17–26. If a man's faith has no moral effect upon him, it is, as James says a "dead" faith. It has not really brought the light and blessing of God's grace into his soul, and of what value is a faith which does not do this? But, on the other hand, it is important to see that the "works" by which a man is justified are not necessarily what men would call "good works" at all. The two examples given prove this very distinctly, for the first is that of Abraham offering up his son, and the second is that of Rahab betraying her country, neither of them very creditable things from man's point of view. The works which justify are those works which FAITH produces, and which evidence that it is an operative principle in the soul of the believer, and not a mere assent to creeds and doctrines. Faith brings the knowledge of God into a man's soul, and this makes him willing to give up what is naturally dear to him—his self-importance, his religious position and reputation in this world, and all the things in which he was most gratified as a natural man. It also breaks the power of those ties and associations which exist among men, and brings a man out of them to take his place with the people of God. Such are the works of faith, by which a man is justified.

There are many who assent to the doctrines of Christianity, or to the creeds of christendom, and they call themselves "believers." They would stoutly maintain, it may be, among other things, the doctrine of "justification by faith." But their faith, such as it is, has no moral effect on them. It does not separate them from the world, or lead them to surrender what is gratifying to them as men in the flesh. They go on with their pleasures, their money-making, their hobbies and ambitions, and with all the social and political engagements of the world. Theirs is a faith without vitality—a faith which is worthless and "dead." It is a very important truth, especially in days when the Christian faith is professed in some form by so many, that a man must be "justified by works."

ACCEPTANCE

It is the privilege of every believer to be consciously in the favour of God—to be in the unclouded light and joy of Acceptance. But, alas! many who are truly converted are not in the enjoyment of this privilege. It may be helpful to consider briefly *why* not.

The things which hinder converted persons from having the light and joy of Acceptance may be classed under the four following heads:—

1. SELF-RIGHTEOUSNESS.
2. SELF-IMPROVEMENT.
3. SELF-GRATIFICATION.
4. SELF-OCCUPATION.

When I speak of *self-righteousness* in this connection I do not mean the proud self-righteousness of the unconverted man. I refer to the very different form of self-righteousness which leads many to doubt their acceptance with God *because of the imperfections which they find in themselves*. You may say, 'But *ought* I not to have misgivings when I find my spirit and the state of my mind so contrary to that which befits a Christian? and when I am conscious of inconsistencies and backslidings?' That you ought to judge yourself, and be humbled before God about these things, is most true; but it is in no wise true that your righteousness and acceptance with God depend upon yourself, or are measured by your condition or conduct. To have such a thought in the mind is really to suppose that you could be in the favour of God by being worthy of that favour in yourself. It is simply *self-righteousness*.

Then souls reason in this way: 'Surely if I were converted I should be very different. There must be a great change in one who is born again. And if I had the Spirit of God He would help me to gain the victory over evil habits—over the lusts and tempers of the flesh—and to become pleasing to God. But instead of this more temptations seem to come in my way than ever before, and the evil tendencies of my heart seem to have acquired greater strength. I never felt more utterly unworthy of God's favour and acceptance.' It is not always easy to see that *self-righteousness* is hidden under all this, yet such is the case. There is the thought that, either by our own efforts, or by God's grace and the help of His Spirit, we should become *in ourselves* suitable to God's favour; and we are disappointed and distressed to find that we make so little progress in this direction.

It is important to know that the effect of the new birth, and of the grace of God, is not to bring about some change in us on which we could rest, but to convince us of the *impossibility* of finding righteousness, or suitability to the favour of God, in ourselves. An unconverted man may think himself worthy of God's favour, but every converted person is made conscious of utter unfitness in himself for that favour. The awakened soul gives account of itself in such language, as, "I have sinned"; "I am undone"; "I am vile"; "I abhor myself." Indeed, it is a common thing for such to suppose that since they turned to God the evil tendencies of their hearts had increased rather than otherwise. The fact is that before conversion we went with the stream, and not a ripple impeded our progress; when, by grace, we made some stand *against* the current, we began to feel its force, and to be distressed by it, as never before.

Now I should like to bring two circles before the consideration of your hearts—a circle of darkness and a circle of light—each having for its centre the Lord Jesus. The thought of the first is presented to us in a solemn way by the words, "Jesus our Lord… who was delivered for our offences" (Romans 4: 25). Here we are brought in view of a circle filled with everything that was due to us. *Our sins*, with all their righteous consequences, are found there; the holy *judgment of God* is there; *death* is there. Everything that attached to us in our responsibility as creatures of Adam's race was taken account of at Calvary. And we see Jesus our Lord—the Holy One of God—in the midst of that circle of darkness, having taken upon Himself by the will of God to remove everything that rendered us liable to divine judgment. He was "delivered for our offences," and He has removed everything which was the outcome and the proof of our lost and guilty state as children of Adam by bearing its full judgment. None could do it but Himself, and He has done it in love, that He might bring divine love to us. Well may we adore His sacred Name for ever.

Thank God! the *darkness* of the cross is for ever past, and *now* as we look there we see *glory* and *love*. We see *the glory of God* there; all that He is in majesty, truth, and holiness, as against sin, is fully declared there; and yet there is the most blessed manifestation of His *love*. Where sin seemed to prevail the glory of redemption is shed.

Now, a new scene opens, as we read, "and was raised again for our justification." An Old Testament saint might stand on a mountain-top, and seeing the landscape blotted out as a dense cloud from the sea rolled over it, might think of the words, "I have blotted out, as a thick cloud, thy transgressions, and, as a cloud, thy sins" (Isaiah 44: 22). As he looked into the distances of space he would be reminded that "As far as the east is from the west, so far hath He removed our transgressions from us" (Psalm 103: 12). He could hardly catch a glimpse of the gleaming snows of Lebanon without thinking of Isaiah 1: 18 or Psalm 51: 7. But for the believer now all these material figures give place to a living Person—a Person in spotless suitability to that new world which He has entered as raised from the dead. Jesus our Lord has been "raised again for our justification." The believer is cleared before God of everything that attached to him in his ruined responsibility in this world, and he is cleared in view of another world, for a *Risen Saviour* is the measure of his justification—*Christ Risen* is his righteousness. The apprehension of this by faith gives peace with God, for we read, 'Therefore being justified by faith, *we have peace with God* through our Lord Jesus Christ' (Rom. 5: 1).

Then a further blessing is brought before us by the words, "By whom also we have access by faith into this grace [favour] wherein we stand" (Rom. 5: 2). No believer would question the fact that the Lord Jesus Christ as the Risen Man is in unclouded favour with God. If He was the Centre of a circle of darkness upon the cross, He is now the Centre of

A CIRCLE OF LIGHT.

How rightly and gloriously does all the light of God's favour shine upon *Him*! It could not be otherwise. The Son of God—the Glorifier of God—

the One who by Himself purged our sins—is unquestionably in the cloudless light of God's favour. Let the believer's heart take in this blessed fact in all its reality and greatness, and then let him be divinely assured that he is entitled to stand in the same favour. A place in that circle of light has been secured by divine grace, and in divine righteousness, for every believer. And it is "by faith" that we appropriate our place in that circle of light, and have "access" into this favour.

Allow me to use a very simple illustration. I was lately in an old English city, and I observed that the principal streets were marked out in squares, and on every square a name was written in large white letters. I asked the meaning of this, and I was told that a fair was to be held shortly in the streets of the city, and that persons had paid for the right to stand during the fair in the square spaces on which their names were written. Now it is a blessed thing to know that Christ has secured for us a standing in that circle of light and favour where He is. To use my illustration, there is a place in that circle of light on which, dear fellow-believer, your name is written. You are entitled to stand there, but it may be that you have never by faith *occupied your standing*. I feel sure that the men whose names I saw written on the ground were not content to know that they had right and title to a standing in the fair. I think I am safe in saying that everyone would be careful to *appropriate* and *occupy* his standing. It is a wonderful moment for the soul when by faith we appropriate and occupy our standing in the favour of God—when we know that we are received by God in all the acceptance of Christ. We do not then think of ourselves, or of our worthiness, at all. We think of CHRIST—His perfections, His suitability to divine favour, His infinite acceptance with God—and by faith we have access into the favour of which He is so worthy.

A second hindrance is that many have not given up the thought of

SELF-IMPROVEMENT,

and this effectually robs them of the joys of acceptance. They know that Christ is their righteousness, and they wish to answer to the amazing grace which has come to them; but they cannot bring themselves up to their idea of what a Christian ought to be. Hence a painful sense of defect is generally present with them; they are self-condemned in so many points that their enjoyment of divine favour is much clouded.

I do not wish to be misunderstood. I am not saying one word against having a high standard before the soul of what a Christian is and ought to be. I would rather earnestly desire to see in the minds of young believers, and of Christians generally, a much more elevated ideal than is commonly cherished. The believer should not allow himself for a moment to accept a lower standard than the full height of Christianity according to God, as we may learn it in the Scriptures. Nor do I say one word against holy self-judgment. I would seek in every way to cultivate divine sensitiveness of conscience—the spiritual ability to recognise and judge whatever is contrary to divine light and love in ourselves.

But *self-disappointment* is a very different thing from *self-judgment*. Indeed, if there were true self-judgment there would never be self-disappointment. If in honesty and sobriety of soul I have judged "that in me, (that is, in my flesh,) dwelleth no good thing," I shall certainly not *expect* anything from myself, and it has been well said that where there is no expectation there can be no disappointment. But I feel sure that many young believers, and I dare say some old ones too, are very familiar with the wretched and depressing experience which I have spoken of as *self-disappointment*. They have made many fresh starts; they have often been stirred up, and have made up their minds to be more for Christ; they have thought, 'I shall do better now; I am more earnest about it than I was before'; but it has all ended in disappointment. They have no idea that they are trying to improve themselves; they would repudiate such a thought; they suppose that they know better than to look for good in themselves; and yet their disappointment is the plain proof that, in spite of all their knowledge of Scripture, they have expected to make themselves different, for they are disappointed because they have not succeeded in doing so.

Let me use another simple illustration. Suppose your neighbour had a heap of rubbish in his garden, and you saw him turning it over very diligently every day and constantly coming away looking very crestfallen and disappointed. You would be sure that he had expected to find something that was worth the search. One day you ask him over the hedge if there is anything valuable in the heap of stuff he has got there. 'Oh, no,' he says; 'it is only rubbish, of no value to me or anybody else.' But the next day you see him turning it over again, and looking as disappointed as ever, and this occurs day after day for weeks. You would think, 'Whatever that man *says*, it is evident he has not given up the expectation of finding something there.'

Many believers are like this. They say that there is no good in themselves, and that they do not expect to find any; but, nevertheless, they suffer a good deal of *self-disappointment* from time to time, and this proves that they have not really given up the thought of *self-improvement*. It is strange that we should be so foolish, in the light of Scripture, and after all the experience we have had.

Let me carry my illustration a little further. One day you see your neighbour applying a lighted match to the heap of rubbish, and then standing by until the whole is consumed to ashes. You stroll down the garden and make some remark about it. He says, 'I can see now what a fool I have been in wasting so much time over this rubbish-heap. The owner of the garden knew all about it, and he told me it was nothing but rubbish, and I proved it to be so every time I turned it over. And yet I must have had an idea there was something good in it, because I was so disappointed to find nothing but rubbish. Now I am glad it is all burned, and I shall waste no more time over it.' You can see now that he not only *says* it is rubbish, but he has *really judged it to be such*, and has given it up as perfectly worthless.

God has judged the flesh absolutely in the death of Christ. "Our old man has been crucified with Him." Before God our whole condition and state as in Adam has come under judgment and is done with. The heap of rubbish is burned; it is cleared away absolutely for God. But there is a needs-be that we should reach in our souls the same conclusion as God—that we should realise the necessity for the complete removal of everything that we are as in the flesh—and that we should rejoice to be clear of it by the death of Christ. If I live to God it is as one completely sanctified by the death of Christ, as entirely clear of everything that the Christian can speak of as his "old man." If I am drawn into the company of Christ it is as one who lives because He lives, as one associated with Him in life. I take account of myself as being 'alive unto God in Christ Jesus.' It is thus that I am in conscious suitability to divine light and love. I am in spirit apart from all the imperfection that attaches to me as in Adam; I do not look for, or desire, any improvement of *that* state; I recognise it as a thing wholly condemned.

On the other hand, my heart is attracted by the perfections and blessedness of that new state in which *Man* is found absolutely suitable to all the thoughts and love of God—a state in which only ONE MAN is yet found actually. The Spirit of God delights to make *that Man* attractive to us, to lead our hearts into the immeasurable satisfaction and good pleasure which God has found in Him, and thus to form in our affections the appreciation of that in which life to God really consists. It is perfectly disclosed in Christ Jesus; our souls learn it adoringly in Him, and thus learning it we are formed in it. I believe if we are responsive to the Spirit of God He will confirm us in utter and unreserved *self-judgment*, but He will lead our hearts into the blessedness of that which is infinitely acceptable to God, as it is found in completeness and perfection in Christ Jesus. And He will lead us into this, not as an unattainable ideal, but *as that in which we live to God*. He is the "Spirit of life in Christ Jesus," and He would form us in the knowledge and appreciation of that which alone is life to God, as set forth in Him, that we might be consciously "in Christ Jesus." Our old state as in Adam is only for us, as it is for God, a condemned thing; and we live to God as "in Christ Jesus," and as spiritually formed in the appreciation of that new state of perfection and of suitability to God's good pleasure which is so gloriously set forth in Him.

I do not say that we fully learn what it is to be "in Christ Jesus" in a moment, but there is a moment when we first take account of ourselves as being alive unto God in Him. There may be growth and enlargement in our apprehension of the character and blessedness of that new state in which Man is found eternally to God's good pleasure. But it is an immense gain to be *on that line* with God, and thus to be delivered from the thought of *self-improvement*.

I believe the third section of my subject brings us face to face with the true reason why many know so little of the joy and liberty of Acceptance. I speak to you as one who has often had to learn by sad experience that

SELF-GRATIFICATION

is a deadly foe of the soul's prosperity. May God hold our consciences in His own presence as we speak of it.

I should like to read two Scriptures which have very pointed reference to this matter. "And they that are Christ's have crucified the flesh with the affections and lusts" (Gal. 5: 24). "Forasmuch then as Christ hath suffered for us in the flesh, arm yourselves likewise with the same mind: for he that hath suffered in the flesh hath ceased from sin; that he no longer should live the rest of his time in the flesh to the lusts of men, but to the will of God" (1 Peter 4: 1, 2).

To *crucify* a man is certainly not to *gratify* him. I suppose every converted person would admit that the flesh is a condemned thing in the sight of God. But if so, it cannot be otherwise than a condemned thing for the Christian. "They that are Christ's" have reached the same judgment of the flesh as God has. It is characteristic of the Christian that he has "crucified the flesh." The Christian is in heart and conscience on that ground—that the flesh is a thing not to be allowed or gratified in any way. And if he is not true to the ground he has taken, *his conscience and his heart condemn him*. He cannot make provision for the flesh, or gratify it in any way, without bringing a cloud over the joy of his acceptance.

Indeed, a certain degree of departure in heart must always *precede* self-gratification. It was at a time of "famine in the land" that "Abram went down into Egypt to sojourn there." It is when, from some unjudged cause, we are not opening our mouths wide and having them filled by the Lord, when we are not fed "with the finest of the wheat" and satisfied "with honey out of the rock," that we are in danger of turning from the Lord, and being given up to our own heart's lust, and to walk in our own counsels. (See Psalm 81.) Beloved brethren, let us watch the *beginnings* of decline, let us make haste to judge the spiritual sloth, the self-confidence, the inward departure from first love that steal almost imperceptibly over our hearts, and prepare us to admit suggestions of self-gratification which would otherwise never approach us.

God graciously furnishes us with many safe-guards. I often think of that verse, "put ye on the Lord Jesus Christ, and make not provision for the flesh, to fulfil the lusts thereof" (Rom. 13: 14). The very fact that we have to make provision before we can "fulfil the lusts" of the flesh is a mercy. It gives us time to take the alarm, and God does not fail to warn us by smitings of heart and conscience. The things that hinder and damage you most are things for which you have to make provision.

The great thing is to meet every proposal of self-gratification *armed with the mind to suffer in the flesh*. Sin is the *gratification* of the flesh, but 'he that hath *suffered* in the flesh hath ceased from sin.' If you allow yourself to entertain a suggestion of self-gratification—if you consider it, and give it a place in your mind—you are done for. You have laid aside your armour, and will fall an easy prey to the foe. But there will be no response to the suggestion or temptation if you stand armed with the mind to *suffer* in the flesh. That which is proposed to you is exactly opposite to what you are set for. It is suggested that you should be *pleased* and *gratified* in that very thing in which you are fully minded to *suffer*. You are now in conflict with sin—not going along with it; you suffer in the flesh, and have "ceased from sin." You no longer live the rest of your "time in the flesh to the lusts of men, but to the will of God."

I must now say a little about the fourth hindrance to which I alluded, viz.:—

SELF-OCCUPATION.

I am sure that this underlies the hindrances which we have already looked at, but there are forms of self-occupation which perhaps hardly fall under the three previous heads, and yet are a withering blight upon the joy of Acceptance. There are four kinds of self-occupation.

1. *Self-occupation as to soul experience*. A beloved servant, now with the Lord, used to say that he never knew souls much occupied with experience—whether that of Rom. 7, Gal. 5, or holiness by faith—that it did not end in making *self* a great object of consideration. Some minds are always attracted by what is experimental. They do not know deliverance, and experimental truths seem to offer that which they are seeking. They are not seeking an increased knowledge of *the Grace of God*, or deepened acquaintance with *Christ*; their object of desire is to have a more satisfactory experience. That is, *self* is still their centre. And such souls are constantly occupied either in bemoaning how little they have got or attained, or in complacently assuming that they have reached a certain stage of experience. It has often been remarked that in the writings of those who advocate 'holiness by faith' the beauty and perfection of what Christ is in Himself as an all-blessing Object for the heart is very little presented. Christ is set forth as *One who can bring about a new experience* in the believer, and it is easy to see that the new experience has often a more prominent place in the mind than Christ.

The remedy for all this is to have *the purpose of God* distinctly in view, and His purpose is to have us before Him 'as sons with Him who is above.' It is

God's pleasure that we should "receive the adoption of sons"—that is, receive the place of sonship as a gift. This is no question of effort, experience, or attainment. It is the glorious purpose of divine love, and infinitely transcends every conception of blessing that could be formed in our minds. No standard of experience, however exalted, and no goal of attainment, however advanced, which we could propose to ourselves could possibly come up to *sonship*. Whatever your ideal may be, the purpose of God eclipses it. Your standard of perfection dims and fades before the glorious light of the divine purpose. Indeed, there is but one Person in whom you can learn the exceeding greatness and blessedness of your place according to the love and purpose of God, and that is the Son of God. God has predestinated us to be "conformed to the image of His Son, that He might be the firstborn among many brethren" (Rom. 8: 29). 'We are sons of God by faith in Christ Jesus,' 'and because we are sons, God has sent forth the Spirit of His Son into our hearts, crying, Abba, Father.' (Gal. 3: 26; 4: 6)

You will find that when souls are occupied with experience—whether it be in connection with holiness, power for service, or spiritual attainment—they always have something before them less than the purpose of God. They are either pursuing, or are satisfied with, something less than that which divine love proposes, and thus they are losers to an incalculable extent. It is when the purpose of God in its greatness is before our hearts, and we are mightily attracted by it, that our experience becomes like that of the beloved servant who could say, "Not as though I had already attained, either were already perfect: but I follow after, if that I may apprehend that for which also I am apprehended of Christ Jesus. Brethren, I count not myself to have apprehended: but this one thing I do, forgetting those things which are behind, and reaching forth unto those things which are before, I press toward the mark for the prize of the high calling of God in Christ Jesus" (Phil. 3: 12–14). This is Christian experience—the experience of a man who was not thinking of his experience, but of the exceeding greatness of *the purpose of God*.

2. *Self-occupation in service*. It is a sad thing when *service* interferes with *soul-prosperity*. Service may take possession of the heart until it becomes the theme of conversation, the subject-matter of correspondence, and the centre round which the thoughts continually revolve. It is possible to be so engrossed with service that one's meditations are coloured by it, one's prayers are full of it, and the Word of God becomes simply a quarry out of which material for sermons and addresses can be dug. This is a serious loss to the soul, and many are thereby hindered from making spiritual progress. Very often young believers who have not even peace with God are encouraged to take up service, and they become so occupied with what they are doing that they are not at leisure to learn or to take their place in the favour of God. Hence, so long as the service prospers, and they get on pretty well with it, they are happy. *The service is their life*. But when there is no success, and the whole thing seems to be a failure, their joy collapses; and they have to discover how little they have really got, and in many cases to find that they are perfect strangers to the liberty and joy of Acceptance.

I feel sure that it is a much greater thing with God that we should be in the enjoyment of peace with Him, in the light of His favour, and in the acceptance of sonship, than that we should be preaching, teaching, or giving away tracts. I do not undervalue service, and I thank God for every true servant, but I am sure that *the first thing in the mind of God* is to bring us *to Himself*—into the enjoyment of His favour, which is better than life—into the real liberty and satisfaction of heart in divine love which is connected with Acceptance. Anything which occupies us so that we are diverted from this is *a positive hindrance*, even if it be a thing apparently so excellent as service.

3. *Self-occupation induced by physical weakness*. Believers with weakly bodies are in special danger of becoming very self-centred. Their condition and circumstances tend to make them very much objects of consideration to themselves. There may be need for great care, for special diet and treatment, and this very often turns to *self-occupation*, and the soul's spiritual joy declines. I dare say some of my hearers have no difficulty in recognising the symptoms of this baneful malady. You would like to know if there is a cure for it. Well, I believe there is. The remedy for this kind of self-occupation is to know the love and support of Christ as Priest. I believe the Priesthood of Christ comes into exercise to sustain us above the self-occupation into which we should otherwise sink. In His love He makes His sympathy a reality to our hearts, and the fact that He considers our trouble and has known our soul in adversity as One touched with the feeling of our infirmities, having been in all points tempted like as we are apart from sin, draws our hearts to Him in a very blessed way. In nearness to Himself we enjoy His love, and are assured of His support, and the moment our hearts come consciously into the circle of His love *self* is no longer the centre. It is in thus drawing our hearts to Himself that Christ succours us. To find that we are objects of consideration to *Him* is an infinite solace, and it brings *Him* before our hearts in such a way that we are sustained above the consideration of ourselves. There is the positive support of *His love*; and thus our weakness becomes the occasion of

proving the personal love and support of Christ, so that we are sustained in the joy of God's favour. We are sensible that we need support—that the love of Christ in this blessed way is an indispensable necessity—but *we may have* the support that we need. The love of Christ makes it available for us; His known love is the sure pledge of it to our hearts. And thus supported by Him, we may have—in spite of much weakness—the unclouded light and joy of God's favour in our souls.

4. *The self-occupation of idleness*. Few things are treated with such severity in Scripture as idleness, and there can be nothing more destructive of all spiritual joy. People who have no particular household or business duties, and who are not engaged in some form of service, are almost invariably self-occupied and unhappy. It is the will of God that men and women should have some form of occupation, and this ordinance of God cannot be set aside without evil results. A good many cases of spiritual depression would be quickly cured by a little more work. It is better to dig in the garden, to chop firewood, or to break stones on the road, than to do nothing.

Then if the Lord has called you to any little service of a more spiritual sort you cannot be negligent or slothful in it without suffering loss in your soul. Devotedness will necessarily produce diligence, and where these are lacking, the light and joy of God's favour are not likely to be the conscious portion of the heart.

It is thus, as having access by faith into the favour of God, as being alive unto God in Christ Jesus, as being armed with the mind to suffer in the flesh, and as delivered from self-occupation of every kind, that we may know what it is, not only to be clear as to the doctrine, but to be in *the light and joy* of Acceptance. God would have us to enjoy His favour, which is better than life, and to know the answer in our souls to the wondrous desire, "that the love wherewith Thou hast loved Me may be in them, and I in them." Thus may we 'find in Abba's favour our spirit's present home.'

DELIVERANCE

Romans 6: 1–23; **7:** 1–25; **8:** 1–39

The subject of Deliverance is one to which our attention has often been directed of late, but its great importance will, I think, justify me in bringing it before you again. And I do so the more willingly because I know it is a subject about which many are exercised. Indeed, I trust we are *all* exercised about it, for not one of us is beyond the need of it. When I speak of Deliverance I do not mean Peace with God. It has frequently been said, 'So-and-so has got deliverance,' when what was meant was that the one in question had entered into peace with God. I do not use the word in this sense, but this will be evident as we proceed.

There are three things from which we need to be delivered in order to have spiritual liberty. They are brought before us in Romans 6, 7, and 8.

1. Sin, or the world.
2. The law.
3. The flesh.

I believe that Romans 6 is regarded by many as a merely doctrinal chapter. So far from this being the case it is a chapter the truths of which all turn upon *affection for Christ*, and a more intensely *practical* chapter it would be difficult to find. It is a chapter that can only be fully appreciated by those in whose hearts the Lord Jesus Christ has acquired a supreme place. Then it is of great moment that we should see how His supremacy in our affections is established. And I think we have a fine illustration of this in the history of Mary Magdalene. Let us read three passages from the Gospels.

"The twelve were with Him; and certain women, which had been healed of evil spirits and infirmities, Mary called Magdalene, out of whom went seven devils" (Luke 8: 1, 2). "And many women were there, beholding afar off, which followed Jesus from Galilee, ministering unto Him: among which was Mary Magdalene" (Matthew 27: 55, 56). "But Mary stood without at the sepulchre weeping: and as she wept, she stooped down, and looked into the sepulchre, and seeth two angels in white, sitting, the one at the head, and the other at the feet, where the body of Jesus had lain. And they say unto her, Woman, why weepest thou? She saith unto them, Because they have taken away my Lord, and I know not where they have laid Him. And when she had thus said, she turned herself back, and saw Jesus standing, and knew not that it was Jesus. Jesus saith unto her, Woman, why weepest thou? whom seekest thou? She, supposing Him to be the gardener, saith unto Him, Sir, if thou have borne Him hence, tell me where thou hast laid Him, and I will take Him away. Jesus saith unto her, Mary. She turned herself, and saith unto Him, Rabboni; which is to say, Master. Jesus saith unto her, Touch Me not; for I am not yet ascended to My Father: but go to My brethren, and say unto them, I ascend unto My Father, and your Father; and to My God, and your God" (John 20: 11–17).

Four steps in soul-history are brought before us in these Scriptures. (1) She was healed; (2) she was in the company of the One who had healed her; (3) she followed Him to *death*—to the end of all hopes and expectations *here*; and (4) she reached Him in another order of things as the Risen One. I would like to use these four steps as illustrative of truths in the epistle before us, though what answers to the last is more properly to be found in Colossians. But using them by way of illustration, I would say that in chapters 3 and 4 we see (1) how we have been "healed"; in chapter 5 we are (2) in the company of the One who has healed us; and in chapter 6 we recognise (3) that *this* is the sphere of death—Christ has *died* here; while (4) on the other hand we come into touch with *life* in being able to account ourselves "alive to God in Christ Jesus." But I must open this out a little more in detail.

1. We learn what has been *done for us*. Christ Jesus has been set forth as a Mercy-seat "through faith in His blood" (Romans 3: 25), and it is by His stripes we are healed (1 Peter 2: 24). By the death of Christ God's righteousness is declared, and He is "just, and the Justifier of him which believeth in Jesus" (Romans 3: 26). The believer's iniquities are forgiven, his sins are covered; God will not impute sin to him, he is justified (Romans 4: 7, 8, 24, 25).

2. We are with One who ministers the favour of God *to us*. I am sure that when He was here He ministered a sense of divine favour to those who were with Him. It was not only that He had done great things *for them* whereof they were glad, but He ministered *to them* the favour of God. They must have known what it was to sit down "under His shadow with great delight," and to find His fruit sweet to their taste. Now in Romans 5 we are brought to the Lord Jesus Christ as the risen and glorified One who ministers the favour of God to the hearts of those who believe on Him. And, beloved brethren, I do not think we can learn the favour of God *apart from Him*. Learning the doctrine of it does not feed the heart. If you want to have the joy of divine favour, you must be *near the One* through whom it is all ministered.

It has often been pointed out that the preposition "*through*" is characteristic of this chapter. There are seven things in the chapter which come to us "*through*" our Lord Jesus Christ. He ministers to us the favour of God in its blessed perfection. (1) 'We have peace with God *through* our Lord Jesus Christ' (verse 1); (2) '*through* whom also we have access by faith into this grace wherein we stand' (verse 2); (3) 'Much more then, being now justified by His blood, we shall be saved from wrath *through* Him' (verse 9); (4) 'we also joy in God, *through* our Lord Jesus Christ' (verse 11); (5) '*through* whom now we have received the reconciliation' (verse 11); (6) 'they which receive abundance of grace, and of the gift of righteousness, shall reign in life *through* One, Jesus Christ' (verse 17); (7) 'that as sin hath reigned unto death, even so might grace reign, through righteousness, unto eternal life, *through* Jesus Christ our Lord' (verse 21). Here we see the scope and fulness of divine favour, and every bit of it, from "peace with God" up to "eternal life," is ministered "through" the risen and glorified Saviour. We only touch the positive blessings of Christianity as we reach HIM. It has sometimes been said that souls may have *blessing* without having the *Blesser*, but this is hardly the truth. Of course one may have a measure of relief and the assurance of eternal security because we trust the precious blood and finished work of Christ, but when we come to divine favour and the positive blessings of Christianity, they are *all* connected *with a* PERSON, *and they are inseparable from that Person*. God would thus connect our every thought of blessing and life with the Lord Jesus Christ, and would lead us into the wondrous thought that *we are bound up with Him*. And the blessings we have as bound up with Him infinitely transcend everything in this world. I am sure that if we esteem the blessing and favour of

God greater than anything on earth, the One who ministers that favour to us must acquire supremacy in our affections. We bow before Him in affection and adoration. He becomes our hearts' 'Object, bright and fair.'

3. Then in chapter 6 we come to the intensely solemn fact that the One who ministers the favour of God to us, and has thus made Himself precious to our hearts, has *died here*. And as we apprehend this great fact we realise that life is not *here*—this is the death sphere. Do you not think the disciples realised this in their hearts when Jesus died? The One who had ministered the favour of God to them, and made Himself everything to them, *went into death*. This is the way in which we reach death *on the privilege line*. That is, as our affections go after Christ we find He is not here—He has died here; and our hearts count it their holy privilege to be associated with Him. 'Know ye not, that so many of us as were baptised unto Jesus Christ were baptised *unto His death*?' (Romans 6: 3).

Before I go further into this, I may say that there is another way of reaching death, and that is on what may be called *the experimental line*. This is brought before us in type in connection with Marah. "So Moses brought Israel from the Red Sea; and they went out into the wilderness of Shur: and they went three days in the wilderness, and found no water. And when they came to Marah, they could not drink of the waters of Marah, for they were bitter: therefore the name of it was called Marah. And the people murmured against Moses, saying, What shall we drink? And he cried unto the Lord; and the Lord showed him a tree, which when he had cast into the waters, the waters were made sweet" (Exodus 15: 22–25).

I am sure we have to learn that death is on things here. We may learn it on the privilege line or on the experimental line, but it must needs be learned. “They went three days in the wilderness, and found no water.” We have to learn that there is nothing *here* to minister to us; there is no refreshment here—not a blade of grass or a drop of water for the lambs and sheep of Christ’s flock. We may think, in our folly, that if we had this or that it would minister satisfaction to us. We may set our eyes on some pleasing prospect; certain things may seem full of promise; we may turn aside to quench our thirst at what appears to be an attractive pool—only to find that it is a delusive mirage. Companionships, hobbies, books, music—or any of the thousand and one things which engage the minds of men—must fail to minister satisfaction to the believer’s heart. God will not have us to find satisfaction in the things which are here.

Then when they came to Marah “they could not drink of the waters of Marah, for they were bitter.” It is the will of God that we should prove that death is *here*. *Life* is in another place, and in connection with another order of things. If there is anything in this world in which we are looking for satisfaction we shall find that, in one way or another, death will come in on it. Sooner or later death touches everything here, and we are made to taste its bitter waters. But, thank God, there is that which enables us to expect and accept death in this world. “The Lord showed him a tree, which when he had cast into the waters, the waters were made sweet.” It is at this point that the privilege line and the experience line meet. In Romans 5 God shows us the Tree, and we sit down under His shadow with great delight, and find His fruit sweet to our taste as He ministers to us the favour of God. But in Romans 6 we see that that lovely Tree has gone into the bitter waters of death. Has God showed you that Tree? Has He attracted your heart to the One who was here as a "tender Plant," as a "Tree planted by the rivers of water," and as a "green olive Tree in the house of God"? I say, has God attracted your heart to that Blessed One in His fruitfulness and beauty—the only lovely and perfect Object ever seen in this wilderness world? Then I am sure you will be deeply affected as you think of *His death*. I feel that one of the greatest needs of our souls is to have more present with us the great fact that the Lord Jesus has *died here*. What an effect it would have upon us! How it would set us apart from things here! How it would bring home to us that *death is here!* Yet we should learn this not as a thing to sorrow over as if we regretted it, but as a privilege, for it is in death that He has brought divine love to us. And we cannot touch *life* without accepting death here. If we are conscious of being bound up with our Lord Jesus Christ, we shall not want to live *where He died*. This is involved, so to speak, in our baptism; we have been baptised "unto His death." The act of baptism is not the important thing for a Christian (though it has its place), but the moment when in heart and spirit he realises what is involved in it and accepts it. We are then prepared for death here; we accept it, for we have been baptised "unto His death."

If Christ has died, it is evident that He is not in things here. "His life is taken from the earth" (Acts 8: 33). Now, beloved brethren, have we enough affection for Him to be willing to "pass over unto the other side"? The truths of Romans 6 turn upon this. It is beautifully illustrated in 2 Samuel 15: 19–22. "Then said the king to Ittai the Gittite, Wherefore goest thou also with us? return to thy place, and abide with the king; for thou art a stranger, and also an exile. Whereas thou camest but yesterday, should I this day make thee go up and down with us? seeing I go whither I may, return thou, and take back thy brethren: mercy and truth be with thee. And Ittai answered the king, and said, As the Lord liveth, and as my lord the king liveth, surely in what place my lord the king shall be, whether in death or life, even there also will thy servant be. And David said to Ittai, Go, and pass over. And Ittai the Gittite passed over, and all his men, and all the little ones that were with him." Here we see one whose heart was so knit to David that in what place David was, "whether in death or life," there would he be. The best place on earth was nothing to him without David; for his heart there was no *life* where David was not. And in this noble language of a devoted heart we have strikingly presented the truth of Romans 6. The great point of the chapter is that it is the believer's privilege to be in the same relation to things as Christ, and where there is true affection for Him this privilege will be appropriated with holy joy. This is how the believer becomes dead to sin.

Another illustration of the same thing can be found in 2 Samuel 19: 24: "And Mephibosheth the son of Saul came down to meet the king, and had neither dressed his feet, nor trimmed his beard, nor washed his clothes, from the day the king departed until the day he came again in peace." In this case the application to ourselves is very distinct and striking, inasmuch as Mephibosheth had not *actually* gone over with David, nor have *we* actually passed out of the sphere of sin and death. But Mephibosheth's *heart* had gone with David; his life was bound up with David, and he had no interest in what was going on in the place where David was not. He would not assert himself, or make anything of himself in Jerusalem; he would only appear there in the character of a mourner. It was, no doubt, a fine time in Jerusalem—people having their grievances redressed and benefits conferred on them by the usurper—but Mephibosheth was dead to it all. For him it was all *sin*, and his affection for David made him dead to it.

I should like to refer to another thing in Mephibosheth's case, because it illustrates an important point in Romans 6. I mean the full and practical acceptance of judgment upon what we may speak of as his "old man." What Ziba said of him so slanderously was just what we might have expected him to say according to nature. "Behold, he abideth at Jerusalem: for he said, Today shall the house of Israel restore me the kingdom of my father" (2 Sam. 16: 3). But Mephibosheth's account of himself and of his father's house is in perfect and beautiful contrast to this. He says, "For all of my father's house were but dead men before my lord the king: yet didst thou set thy servant among them that did eat at thine own table" (2 Sam. 19: 28). It is lovely to see him acknowledging that death was upon him as of his father's house. Nor does he wish it otherwise, for all the associations and interests of his life had been transferred to another centre. All that was *life* in his estimation was bound up with David. He lived not as of the household of Saul, but by David's grace; his life was in those things which were ministered to him by David. There was not the smallest disposition on his part to allow the activity of that which he recognised as being under death.

In Romans 6: 6 we see what answers to this for ourselves. 'Knowing this, that our old man is crucified with Him, that the body of sin might be annulled, that henceforth we should not serve sin.' As children of Adam we "were but dead men," and we rejoice to know that *before God* our history as belonging to that race has terminated. "Our old man has been crucified with Him." But this is a fact with an intensely practical bearing, for when it is really accepted the body of sin is annulled, and henceforth we do not serve sin. That is, when we recognise that as children of Adam we are under judgment, and that we have gone from the eye of God in judgment, the body of sin is annulled for our hearts. That life in which the totality of sin is found is recognised by us as a condemned thing. And when this is the case its power over our hearts is annulled. Mephibosheth recognised that as of the house of Saul he was under death, and the power of every motive connected with his position in that house was thus annulled for his heart. He was no longer controlled by those motives; he no longer served sin.

The enjoyment of David's grace and responsive affection for David sustained him in complete separation of heart from every motive that would have been natural to him as of the house of Saul. And it is not otherwise with ourselves. The knowledge of doctrine gives no power. One might be very well up in the doctrine of deliverance, and know absolutely nothing of its reality and power. It is as our hearts are under the sway of that grace which is ministered to us through our Lord Jesus Christ, and as we are knit to Him in affection, that we touch and taste a new life, and are severed in heart from everything that constituted the life of "our old man." Thus the body of sin is annulled for our hearts, and we do not henceforth serve sin.

It is important to see that "sin" is used in Romans 6 in a very wide sense, as setting forth the whole circle of things in which the will of man acts. Indeed, "sin" in Romans 6 is almost the same thing as "the world" in 1 John 2. *The world* is that great moral system of which man's will is the animating principle. It is a very solemn thing to see that there is but one thing in which man glories, and that is the power to carry out his own will. If it is only a child acting in known disobedience, he glories in it because it is *his will* to do it. Ambition is the highest form of the same thing. An ambitious man would like to be monarch of the whole world just because it would give *his will* the greatest scope to act. The root principle of politics is the will of man. I admit that Parliament may make laws which benefit men, but they are all put in force on the principle that it is the will of man to have them so. Now, dear brethren, it is of vital importance that we should recognise that the action of the creature's will is *sin*. It is that upon which the judgment of God rests, and which is under death. And this is the reason why man fears death. It is that awful moment when his will can act no longer. Then there is an end of all his glory, for it is the sad and fearful truth that *sin is the only glory of man*.

Now think of what it must have been to the blessed Lord to come into a world of creatures whose very glory it was to carry out their own will. He was indeed a "Man of sorrows," as the prophet so touchingly says, and He could not be otherwise in such a world. I do not think we can conceive what it was to Him—whose meat and drink, whose delight it was to do the will and to seek the glory of God—to be in a world where everyone gloried in his own will. That Blessed One shone amid the darkness of this world in unique and heavenly lustre, the solitary Object of God's delight, the One on whom the eye of God could rest in infinite complacency and satisfaction, the One to whom He could say, "Thou art my beloved Son; in Thee I am well pleased" (Luke 3: 22). He was as little *of* the world when He was here as He is now, but He was *in* it. There was no moral link between Him and the sphere of sin. He was as distasteful to the world as the world was distasteful to Him. The sphere of the glory of man could not tolerate Him, and as soon as God allowed the will of man to act they cast Him out. His death has brought out in strong relief the fact that there is a great gulf between Christ and this world—death is between Him and everything in the sphere of sin. "For in that He died, He died unto sin once."

I need hardly point out that His death is not here

looked at as being *for* sin. It is not atonement which is presented to our thoughts in *this* Scripture. We find the atoning character of Christ's death abundantly in other Scriptures; but here His death is viewed as that which has entirely and for ever separated Him from the sphere of sin. We read in John's gospel of His death as the hour when "He should depart out of this world unto the Father" (John 13: 1); and He said, "If ye loved Me, ye would rejoice, because I said, I go unto the Father" (John 14: 28). His death, in this sense, must have been an unspeakable relief to His spirit. While He was here He was in the presence of sin: all its miseries and woes pressed upon His spirit; while the haughtiness and pride of vain-glorious man, boasting in that which was really his shame, must have filled His heart with a sorrow which we, with minds familiarised with sin, can little understand. What He felt in the presence of the sorrows of this scene we may see in the tears of Bethany, and what He felt in regarding the pride of man we may learn from His weeping over Jerusalem. But He has left the whole scene of man's will; He has died unto sin.

And now for the believer the world is marked by *the absence of Christ*. Sin is there—the will of a fallen creature—and death is there; but *Christ is not there*, and affection for Him is the real power of deliverance from the world. We turn from it because CHRIST is not there. Beloved young Christian, surely you do not want to go on with things in which CHRIST has no place or part? Am I not right in saying that you desire to know more of Him, and of your association with Him who "in that He liveth, He liveth unto God"? I am sure that if we know what it is to be bound up with Him, and to have all our thoughts of blessing and life connected with Him, we shall count it a most precious privilege to be in the same relation to things as He is. Affection for Christ would draw us after HIm to the sphere in which He lives unto God, and this would result in a clean break with the world. We should be able to take account of ourselves as being 'dead unto sin.'

This chapter, which states so plainly that He has died to sin, brings with equal distinctness before us the circle in which He lives. "Christ was raised up from the dead by the glory of the Father" (verse 4). The sphere of man's glory has refused and rejected Him, but the glory of the Father has raised and received Him. These are the two great moral circles brought before us in Romans 6. These circles subsist today, and *death rolls between them*. Now, I ask, in which circle is your life? Are you drawn in affection to Christ in that new world of light and love where He lives unto God? Can you say that you know what it is to be bound up with Him? Then I am sure the power of the world is broken for your heart. For you could not be drawn to Him without finding His death between you and the whole sphere of sin. You could not be drawn to Him without having in your soul something of what Paul expressed when he said, "God forbid that I should glory, save in the cross of our Lord Jesus Christ, whereby the world is crucified unto me, and I unto the world" (Gal. 6: 14). And the one of whom this is true is dead to sin. He would take as little interest in what is going on in the sphere of man's will as Mephibosheth took in what was going on in Jerusalem in the absence of David. It is in the power of affection for Christ that we can reckon ourselves 'to be dead unto sin, but alive unto God in Christ Jesus our Lord.'

We are not "dead to sin" by faith, or by the mere acceptance of truths and doctrines. It is as the Spirit of God attaches us in affection to Christ in the place where He is that we discern the true character of everything here. We see the world in its true colours as the sphere of sin, and we are dead to it. Our *life* is not in that sphere, it is bound up with Christ, and we can in simplicity of heart take account of ourselves as being 'dead unto sin, but alive unto God in Christ Jesus our Lord.' It is not an artificial reckoning, but a simple spiritual reality. And the secret and power of it is affection for Christ.

The practical effect of this is that we are here only for the will of God. We take up our responsibilities and relationships in this world on an entirely new principle. We yield ourselves "unto God, as those that are alive from the dead," and our "members as instruments of righteousness unto God" (verse 13). The effect of His grace reigning in our hearts, and of Christ being supreme in our affections, is that we are won for God, and *His will becomes our glory*. This necessarily involves a clean break with the world in heart and spirit. The believer cannot be entirely separate from "the fornicators of this world" so long as he is in the world; he may have to work among ungodly men, or live in a family where he is the only one converted. But he is morally separated from everything around him by the entire difference of the motives that control him. And he refuses to be identified with anything in which he cannot recognise the will of God. For that which is not the will of God is the will of man, and this, as we have already seen, is sin. Thus the believer walks even as Christ walked. In the midst of a dark scene, where the will of man marks everything, he shines as a light—doing the will of God as one set free from the dominion of sin by being brought under the sway of Grace. "For sin shall not have dominion over you: for ye are not under the law, but under grace" (verse 14).

II. DELIVERANCE FROM LEGALITY.

It would hardly be of much interest to an unconverted man, or to a worldly believer, to unfold how we are delivered from the law. The soul must, in some measure at least, be in the good of what is presented in chapter 6 before it would be prepared to appreciate the aspect of Deliverance which is brought before us in chapter 7. There would be found in anyone who was really 'in the seventh of Romans' an intense separation from the world, a holy abhorrence of sin, and a vehement desire to do the will of God. The will of God has become the glory and delight of his heart; sin is no longer any glory or pleasure to him. Now his distress and complaint is that he finds himself perfectly incapable of carrying out that on which his heart is set. He finds himself altogether incompetent for the will of God, though it commands both his conscience and his heart. But this helplessness arises from the fact that he is under the law, and therefore in his conscience, on the ground of a man living in the flesh; for "the law hath dominion over a man as long as he liveth." It is the supposed case of one who is set for the will of God; but who is, as to his consciousness, *dissociated from Christ*. From the seventh verse to the twenty-fourth there is no mention of Christ, and, so far as the soul's consciousness is concerned, there might be no such Person in existence. Hence there is absolute weakness, no fruit for God, and the soul can only cry, "O wretched man that I am!" Here we see the realisation of those words of Christ, "without Me ye can do nothing" (John 15: 5). I will now seek to show the way of deliverance from this legal bondage.

It is important to observe that the apostle, in writing as he does in this chapter, has Jewish believers specially in view: that is, those who had been under the law, for he says: "I speak to them that know the law" (verse 1). It was most essential *for such* to know the divine way of deliverance from the law, for they had been put under it by God, and a divinely created obligation could only be set aside in a divine way. The apostle recognises that the bond between the law and those who were under it was as inviolable as the marriage bond, which he takes up as an illustration. That is, *death alone could annul it*. If God has put a man under the law, the law will have dominion over him "as long as he liveth."

But death *has* come in. Christ was "come under law," and fulfilled it perfectly in His holy life, and on the cross He bore its curse for those who were under it. But when His dead body hung upon the cross He had passed out of the condition of life to which law applied. We saw in the previous chapter that He died to *sin*, and it is just as true that He has died to *the law*. And we have "become dead to the law by the body of Christ" (verse 4). The principle of being in the same relation to things as Christ is, applied to sin in chapter 6, is here seen to be the believer's privilege in respect of the law. But in this case it is not only a privilege that may be entered upon, but it is the place in which the believer is set by an act of God. "Ye also are become dead [or, have been made dead] to the law by the body of Christ." The law and those who were under it had been joined together by God, but death had come in and the bond is severed. So that 'now we are delivered from the law, having died in that in which we were held' (verse 6).

If this was so in the case of those who had been put under the law by God, it must be perfectly evident that Gentile believers are not under the law. If God takes pains to show us that the bond is dissolved where it did exist, we may be quite sure that no such bond has been formed in the case of Gentile believers who had never been under the law. We are not come to mount Sinai, but to mount Zion. "Ye are not under the law, but under grace."

But there is no *power* in the fact that we have become dead to the law. It is a great thing to see that we are not, in God's account, associated with that which could only demand and exact without conferring upon us any ability to answer to its claims. But to see this is not enough to deliver us from legality in our own spirits. The *power* of deliverance from legality lies not in the dissolution of the old bond, but in the apprehension of a new bond formed in divine grace *between Christ and the soul*: "That ye should be married to Another, even to Him who is raised from the dead, that we should bring forth fruit unto God" (verse 4). Hence, as I have said, this aspect of deliverance, like the first, turns upon the place CHRIST holds in our hearts.

I will take for granted that we rejoice in the fact that we are under obligation to the will of God, and that we also recognise that we have "become dead to the law by the body of Christ." Now it becomes a matter of the greatest interest to us to know *how the will of God comes to us*. The answer is very simple and blessed. It comes to us in CHRIST. We do not acquire our knowledge of what is pleasing to God through the law, but by being brought under the sway of *Christ*—by being "married to Another, even to Him who is raised from the dead."

Three things present themselves at once to the mind in connection with the figure which is here used. A wife would count upon having the *company*, the *love*, and the *support* of her husband. Now connect these three thoughts with the Scripture before us. To be married to Christ is to have *His company*, the enjoyment of *His love*, and the constant assurance of *His support*. I will seek to unfold this a little.

I should like to make clear, in the first place, what I mean by *the company of Christ*. The great beauty and power of the gospels, to my mind, lies in the fact that through them we can be, so to speak, near to that Blessed One. The evangelists present Him to us in the scenes and at the time when He put Himself near to men. And I believe God has given us the Gospels that we might find ourselves near to Him, and learn what He was in the midst of His little company of disciples. We find Him here with those who were much like ourselves. The spiritual dullness, the weakness, yea, and the self-confidence which we find in ourselves we may see also in them. On their side the one bright feature was that they were bound to Him *in affection*, and to His heart, and to the Father's heart, this was everything. He "rejoiced in spirit," even at a moment when His rejection by the world was most manifest, to know that these few "babes" had seen something of His worth; and He could say at another time, 'The Father Himself loveth you, *because ye have loved Me*.' On His side, there was a love that nothing could stay. Faithfulness was there too, but it was the faithfulness of an all-prevailing love. Beloved brethren, it is a wonderful study for our hearts, to see what He was with His own here. To be thus in His company, so to speak. Not reading the Gospels merely as a history, but following that Blessed One in His pathway here, beholding His service of grace and listening to His words, that we may make acquaintance with Him. The apostles had this privilege *immediately*, but we have it *mediately* through their inspired writings. As John says, "That which we have seen and heard declare we unto you, that ye also may have fellowship with us" (1 John 1: 3). In this way God would lead our hearts into company with Christ, and I am sure this would be a good cure for legality, for we could not be near Him without learning *His love*, and a heart breathing the atmosphere of divine love could not be legal.

How did John learn the love of Christ? Surely by being with Him. The planet Mercury is not often seen because it is so near the sun, but when we do get a glimpse of it it is very bright. John is like that planet; we do not see much of him, but when he does appear it is in the bright light of the love of Christ. He was "that disciple whom Jesus loved." Who would not covet to share his place? Thank God, it is open to all.

I have spoken of the way in which we may get near to the Lord, and learn His love to His own, through the Gospels. But I would not have you forget that His death came in, and was the crowning expression of His love. He could say, "Greater love hath no man than this, that a man lay down his life for his friends" (John 15: 13). And we know Him now on the other side of death. The same blessed Person, with unchanged love for His own, but in a new condition. Every natural link with Israel severed, and all association even with His own after the flesh terminated in His death, He is known now outside everything that is of the present order of things. He is dead to sin and the law; we cannot bring Christ into association with things here, or with anything that pertains to man after the flesh. He has died to everything of that kind, and we are married to Him as the One "who is raised from the dead."

In the company of Christ we learn His love, and as we know His *love* we can count on His *support*. Do you not think John could have counted on the support of the One whose love he knew so well? If he had a need or a consciousness of weakness, do you not think he could have *counted* on that Blessed One affording him all the support he needed? If we knew His love better we should be assured that we might count on Him for *everything*. And with a sense of this in our hearts how could we be *legal*? We should know that there could not arise any exigency or need in our path, there could be no weakness in ourselves which would not be an opportunity to prove how His love and power would support us. It is only as we are maintained in this assurance that we are kept free from legality. Believers say, 'I got deliverance ten years ago.' My brother, have you walked in liberty of heart *today*? Have you been maintained in the consciousness of Christ's love and support *today*? What is the good of deliverance if you are not maintained in the power of it? If you get in spirit *dissociated from Christ*, you will find that you are powerless for the will of God. And many a believer who has known something of deliverance has the present experience of one who cries, "O wretched man that I am!" *Dissociated from Christ* I am as helpless as ever.

It is in the company of *Christ* that we learn the will of God. The pleasure of God is fully set forth in Him, and as we are in His company we learn our obligations in the presence of love that we can count upon to support us. The legal believer has a greater sense of the divine claim than he has of divine support, and hence his life is an effort, and he is always more or less under a cloud, because he does not find himself equal to his obligations. The spiritual believer, on the other hand, has a greater sense of divine support than he has of the divine claim upon him, for he knows what it is to be married to Christ, he knows that he can count upon the all-sufficient support of Christ for everything that is the will of God. And thus he is kept in real liberty of heart.

If we get dissociated in spirit from Christ, the more we read the Scriptures, and the more intelligence we get as to the will of God, the more legal we shall become. I do not believe that God would have us to read His Word, if I may so say, *apart from Christ*. He would keep the Scriptures always connected in our hearts *with Christ*. A simple illustration may convey my meaning. I might read a letter written by a husband to his wife, and find much instruction and good counsel in it, but I am sure the wife to whom it was written would read it with a very different feeling. She would read it in the light of *her husband's love*, and it would command her heart. This is how God would have us read the Scriptures. This would preserve us from legality, and it would also give living interest to the Word of God. It would all become to our hearts the expression of His loving thought and care for us. You could not be indifferent to the first epistle to the Corinthians, for instance, when you read, 'the things that I write unto you are *the commandments of the Lord*' (1 Cor. 14: 37). You would not neglect the Revelation so much, perhaps, if you had weighed the fact that it is "The Revelation *of Jesus Christ*, which God gave unto Him, to show unto His servants things which must shortly come to pass" (Rev. 1: 1). It is all put in touch with the One who loves us.

We have an illustration of what it is to be married to Christ in the case of Ruth. There was a kinsman who was willing to redeem Ruth's inheritance, but he could not perform a husband's part to Ruth. This is like the law—willing to take all it can get, but unable to render any support. Boaz, on the other hand, was able and willing to take Ruth, and to put the strong arm of his loving support round her. Christ is the true Boaz. There is an intense desire in the heart of Christ that we should know all that He can be *for us* in the way of strength and support, and in proportion as we enter into this we shall be here *for Him*. If He says to us, "Thou shalt abide for me," He also says, "so will I also be for thee." And the result would be that in liberty of heart we should "bring forth fruit unto God," and we should be perfectly free from legality.

III. DELIVERANCE FROM THE FLESH.

We come now to the third part of our subject; that is, deliverance from the flesh. It is possible to make a distinction between "sin" and "the flesh," because innocent Adam was in flesh without sin. The Lord Jesus, too, was in flesh without sin. But by the fall that terrible principle of evil, which had already manifested itself in the devil and other spiritual beings, came into connection with flesh, and flesh became "sinful" (Rom. 8: 3). *Sin* has become characteristic of the state and condition in which we are found as Adam's children in this world. Hence the expression "the flesh" is frequently used in Scripture to convey in one brief and striking term the thought of all that is morally connected with us as children of fallen Adam. Now the question is, How can we be completely superior to it? We shall find from the chapter before us that the power of deliverance from the flesh lies in the Spirit of God.

The first verse of the chapter (Rom. 8) is of the deepest importance, as indicating how alone the believer can be clear of condemnation. "There is, therefore, now no condemnation to them which are in Christ Jesus." It is not exactly here the condemnation of God that is in question, but condemnation in one's own soul. The believer takes the ground with God of one who is in spirit completely apart from all the imperfection that attached to him as in the flesh. He recognises that not one whit of the flesh will do for God, and that he can only be with God according to the state and acceptance of another Man, even Christ Jesus, in which state and acceptance there is no flaw, but the most complete suitability to the thoughts and love of God. So long as the believer is in his conscience "in the flesh" he is under the law, and therefore under a sense of condemnation.

Then from verse 3 we learn that the law was incapable of giving effect to the pleasure of God. "For what the law could not do, in that it was weak through the flesh, God, sending His own Son in the likeness of sinful flesh, and for sin, condemned sin in the flesh." The law could neither put the flesh right, nor remove it for the glory of God. The first was impossible, but the second has been accomplished in the death of Christ, and it is on this ground that the Spirit is given to believers. God has condemned sin in the flesh. The flesh is a condemned thing, and, as far as God is concerned, it has *gone* from His eye in judgment. Now the Spirit is given to set us on another line altogether, and to form us in an entirely new state. And as we are formed in that new state, we are necessarily delivered from what was characteristic of our old state. I can only now ask you briefly to consider three points in the chapter.

"That the righteousness of the law might be fulfilled in us, who walk not after the flesh, but after the Spirit. For they that are after the flesh do mind the things of the flesh; but they that are after the Spirit, the things of the Spirit" (verses 4, 5). It must be apparent to all that tastes and motives which are formed by the Spirit are necessarily quite diverse from the tastes and motives of the flesh. Now I could not conceive such a thing as a Christian having the Spirit without having a wholly new set of tastes and motives. You see the proof of this in every good convert. He has acquired new tastes; he loves the Word of God, and prayer, and the company of the saints; and he abhors the things that formerly were his greatest gratification. The truth is, though he may know nothing of the doctrine of it, he is now walking according to the Spirit, and is maintained in superiority to the flesh.

The Christian, as such, is 'according to the Spirit.' His desires, motives, and tastes are entirely new. He no longer "minds" the things of the flesh; they are no longer objects of desire or pursuit with him; but as he formerly minded those things so he now minds the things of the Spirit. If a man has a taste for horses, pictures, or music, he minds those things. He makes them his object; he seeks them; he goes where they are to be seen or heard; he is characterised by the things for which he has a taste. And, as a rule, a man of the world will make everything bend to the gratification of his tastes. Now those who are according to the Spirit mind "the things of the Spirit." I suppose many here know what it is to come into an entirely new world of interests and affections, and in minding these new things to find the power and control of the old tastes completely broken. This is the way of deliverance from the flesh.

But it may be said that there are many who profess to be converted in whom these new tastes are very feeble, and for whose hearts the "things of the Spirit" do not seem to have much attraction. Well, this is very sad, but it is easy to account for it. It will be found that in the majority of such cases peace with God is not known, and what such souls need is the ministry of the Gospel of the Grace of God in power to their hearts. The truth is their hearts are not really won for God, and they are not in the enjoyment of His grace. Then, no doubt, there are many cases where the Spirit is so grieved and hindered that souls have hardly any of the good of His presence. If you are going on with the world, or there is a want of uprightness about you, your spiritual development will be greatly impeded. In such a case the Christian is not true to his colours; he is not true to his proper character; *practically* he is more "after the flesh" than "after the Spirit," and this is not Christianity at all. He is one to whom it might well be said, "now it is high time to awake out of sleep."

It is of great importance to "mind" the things of the Spirit. If your spiritual tastes are feeble, it is probably because you cultivate them so little. I have heard believers complain that they had not much desire for the Word of God and prayer, and I have often found in such cases that story books and religious novels were being read with avidity. You will never make any headway until you break with this kind of thing. Minding the "things of the Spirit" will bring you into touch with your brethren, and you will find that there are many whose hearts are, through grace, after those things. And in this way we come into a new circle, outside everything that is of the flesh, where divine affections are found. We love the brethren; the saints become to us the excellent of the earth; and thus, in the exercise of those affections which are of the divine nature, we find deliverance from the flesh.

"But ye are not in the flesh, but in the Spirit, if so be that the Spirit of God dwell in you" (verse 9). Here we see how entirely new is *Christian state*. The Christian is "not in the flesh, but in the Spirit." The fact that the Spirit of God dwells in him is the proof that, for God, the flesh is completely set aside. God could not recognise the flesh in any way, and the fact that His Spirit dwells in the believer is the sure evidence that according to God the believer is no longer "in the flesh." This is the new state of the Christian; he is in the Spirit. According to his divine state the Spirit of God characterises him and not the flesh. *Practically* he is formed in this new state as he walks according to the Spirit. As he cultivates and ministers to those tastes which are of the Spirit, they become increasingly characteristic of him. A taste may be feeble to begin with, but if it is cultivated it becomes characteristic. I am sure that the youngest believer in whom the Spirit dwells *has divine tastes*. There is affection for Christ and for His own in his heart, and at least some degree of desire after His things. It may be that, like the faculties of a child, these things are not much developed as yet; they need to be fed and cultivated; but these things constitute the elements of your new state, and it is in the minding of these things that you will find practical deliverance from the flesh.

"Therefore, brethren, we are debtors, not to the flesh, to live after the flesh. For if ye live after the flesh, ye shall die: but if ye through the Spirit do mortify the deeds of the body, ye shall live" (verses 12, 13). We are under no kind of obligation to the flesh; we recognise it as a condemned thing; and as we walk according to the Spirit in the exercise of spiritual tastes, and in the activity of divine affections, we are able by the Spirit to put to death the "deeds of the body." Thus walking in love and holiness, we are maintained in superiority to all the evil that naturally attaches to us as children of Adam. "Through the Spirit" we are enabled to refuse the flesh, because our life and interests are in another order of things. In short, we have touched a circle of things where *life* is found, and we do not wish to return to that which is morally *death*. It is thus, as giving no quarter to the flesh, that we are found in the liberty of life. "For as many as are led by the Spirit of God, they are the sons of God. For ye have not received the spirit of bondage again to fear; but ye have received the Spirit of adoption, whereby we cry, Abba, Father" (verses 14, 15). Instead of having his life in the circle of pride and self-gratification, where alone the flesh can move, the Christian *lives* in a circle of divine affections, and in the power and enjoyment of that which is truly life he is able to put to death the deeds of the body. And in this way he is practically delivered from the flesh.

In conclusion, it must be remembered that this three-fold cord of deliverance has to be woven together in the soul. Deliverance from sin, the law, and the flesh, are presented to us separately in these Scriptures for our spiritual apprehension, but they are not so much three distinct things as three parts of one whole.

And it must also be remembered that deliverance is a thing which has to be maintained. The very nature of the thing in itself should make this evident, and yet some have spoken of deliverance as if it was something they got years ago, and had never needed to think about since. If I am worldly, or legal, or carnal today, of what good is it to say that I have deliverance? To do so is to turn a great spiritual reality into an empty word. It is only as we are maintained by the Spirit in dependence and divine affections that deliverance will be a present reality to us.

THIRSTING OR OVERFLOWING

Psalm 42: 1–11; **45:** 1–17

I have no doubt that these Psalms give us very distinctly the experience and joy of the remnant of Israel in a day that is yet to come—their experience as disinherited and driven out of the place of privilege, and the subsequent joy of heart with which they will turn to their once-rejected Messiah and find supreme satisfaction in Him and in the anticipation of His reign. But I should like to say a few words at this time on these Psalms in connection with the fact that they bring before us two very distinct states of soul-experience. Nothing could be more striking than the difference between them. In the one we find a soul "thirsting," in the other a heart "overflowing." Psalm 42 answers to "If any man thirst"; while Psalm 45 answers to "He that believeth on Me, as the Scripture hath said, out of his belly shall flow rivers of living water" (John 7: 37, 38).

It is a home question for every one of us, Am I "thirsting" or "overflowing"? Which of the two Psalms is more truly descriptive of the experience of my soul? It is our true blessedness to have CHRIST so before us that our hearts are really *satisfied*. There is satisfaction of which the Lord spoke to the woman at Sychar's well when He said, "whosoever drinketh of the water that I shall give him shall never thirst" (John 4: 14). It should be a cheer to the most tried and disappointed heart in this company to know that there is a satisfaction to be had of such a wonderful nature. So that instead of the murmurs of the wilderness being in the heart and on the tongue, the glories, perfections, and love of Christ so fill the heart that when the mouth opens streams of refreshing and gladness flow forth as in Psalm 45.

I trust every heart here covets to be in this blessed satisfaction. All the instinctive desires of the one born of God, and all the leadings of the Holy Ghost, must be in this direction, and I trust that every such exercise may be deepened in our souls. For there is no royal road by which we can travel into this blessedness without exercise. It sounds very easy and simple to say, 'You must not be self-occupied, you must be occupied with Christ,' but it is not always so easy to act on this oft-repeated advice. Some of the most acute spiritual distress that I have met with has been in souls who were most anxious to be 'occupied with Christ,' and whose great grief was that, in spite of much prayer and effort, they were painfully conscious of being 'self-occupied.' There must be the learning of what self is; the exercise must be gone through in one form or another; but it is an immense encouragement to know that *God* has taken us up that He might deliver us, and introduce our hearts into the blessedness of conscious association with Christ. Would to God that we were a little more earnest in our desire to enter into the purpose of His love, for if there were a little desire on our part there would be a great answer of blessing on God's part.

In Psalm 42 we have a soul in downright earnest. "As the hart panteth after the water brooks, so panteth my soul after Thee, O God. My soul thirsteth for God, for the living God." If this is the language of your heart, there is great blessing in store for you. When believers are being turned upside down and inside out they are apt to be much discouraged, and to have their souls "disquieted" in them. But even amid the exercise God would give us the encouragement of knowing that He has taken us up to bring us into inconceivable blessing. "Hope thou in God," says the psalmist to his soul, "for I shall yet praise Him, who is the health of my countenance."

We *must* travel through these exercises, for the simple reason that *if Christ is to be everything self must be nothing*, and it is oftentimes a long journey to reach this point in the history of the soul. God has to bring self down to nothingness; and though the flesh can do very well with addition or multiplication, it has a strong objection to subtraction and reduction, and will never tolerate being made into a cipher. Hence the long, dreary, and painful years of 'self-occupation' through which most believers drag their slow steps of spiritual progress. One point after another of self-sufficiency and self-importance has to be attacked and reduced, until at length the believer is brought—to use a phrase much more familiar than the experience which it describes—to the end of himself.

We may fix firmly in our minds the fact that 'self' is the great hindrance to Christ in our souls. It may be good self or bad self, carnal self or legal self, worldly self or religious self, but it is *self* in some form that is before us, if Christ is not everything to us, and if our souls are not in the overflowing satisfaction of conscious association with Him. Now in Psalm 42 we see the psalmist allowed to pass through circumstances which reduced him very much. I do not mean to suggest that we find here the full exposure of the flesh. That could not come out until the cross. But we do see the psalmist reduced to extremity, and brought to nothing as to all that he was in himself, and that is the stepping-stone into the blessedness of Psalm 45, where Christ is everything and fills the heart.

There are many ways in which the soul learns the worthlessness of self. No one could be converted without learning *something* of what he was as in the flesh; and the young convert with his desires for holiness and his Spirit-wrought longings after Christ, finds himself in a school where he learns many lessons of the same nature. But perhaps no way could be more humbling—or more efficacious, if the exercise is gone through with God—than the one brought before us in this Psalm. Here we do not find the thirst of the awakened sinner, or of the one who has never tasted that the Lord is gracious, but the thirst of the soul that has lost what it once enjoyed. The psalmist looks back to seasons of holy joy in the past. "When I remember these things, I pour out my soul in me: for I had gone with the multitude; I went with them to the house of God, with the voice of joy and praise, with a multitude that kept holyday."

If you have received "the word of truth, the gospel of your salvation," and thus been brought to know the Lord Jesus as your risen and triumphant Saviour, I am quite sure you have known what it was to have great joy in your soul. When you saw that your sins were all put away, and that God imputed righteousness to you—righteousness the measure and expression of which is Christ risen—you entered into peace with God through our Lord Jesus Christ, and received the Spirit, who shed the love of God abroad in your heart. I dare say many here can remember the deep joy that filled their hearts when the power and preciousness of the gospel first came home to them. I speak not of the awakening of the conscience, nor of the relief and assurance with which many are content, for neither of these gives the joy of God's salvation. I speak of the moment when Christ Risen is really apprehended as the measure and expression of our righteousness, and of our title to stand in the favour of God. Such a moment is one of supreme joy. It could not be otherwise, for at that moment *we measured everything by Christ*. We were happily and completely taken outside ourselves both for righteousness and title to stand in God's favour. We sang with triumph of His love, we exulted in His grace, and in some true, if small, measure we did "joy in God, through our Lord Jesus Christ." How bright the meetings seemed, because we were bright ourselves. How attractive the children of God were to us, for we looked at them all in the light of the grace we had just learned for ourselves. We went with them "with the voice of joy and praise."

But is it not true that for some hearts here this joy of God's salvation, this rapture of "first love," has passed away and left 'an aching void'? They are *thirsting* now rather than *overflowing*. With some it is an eager thirst, for they have hope and faith in God for a divine answer to the longings of their souls. With others, perhaps, almost a despairing thirst, for years of exercise seem to have brought them no nearer to the deliverance they seek. While a larger class have accepted their present condition as being inevitable, and have settled down to take things as they are, and to comfort themselves with the thought of being very happy by-and-by in heaven, and with these the thirst is so feeble that it can hardly be called a thirst at all.

It may be well at this point to consider two questions which naturally suggest themselves in connection with this subject. (1) Is it absolutely necessary for one to go through an experience of this kind after he finds peace? (2) *Why* is such an experience necessary? With regard to the first of these questions, it may be remarked that some souls go through a much deeper process of self-knowledge *before* they enter into peace than do others; and in cases where this exercise had been very deep, and the soul had been under legal preaching, peace and deliverance might be entered into almost simultaneously. But when the gospel has been fully and clearly presented souls are often brought into peace thereby, and then *afterwards* have to learn experimentally what they are as in the flesh. In answer to our second question, it may be said that our hearts have a continual tendency to make *self* the centre. Even when, by God's converting grace, we no longer make self the object of carnal gratification or of religious exaltation, we may, and do, make self the centre of the blessings which God's grace has conferred. We can all remember that it was so with us in the beginning. We thought and spoke much of *our* blessings, of what *we* had got, of what God had done for *us*. I am not at all objecting to this; it is, if I may so say, natural to the infancy of the soul. It gladdens our hearts to hear the young convert speak of the blessings he has got, and of his newfound joy in those blessings; but we can often see very distinctly that he is wrapping all these blessings of grace round himself, and we feel pretty sure that he will have to learn some lessons presently that will take the shine out of him. He will have to learn what a poor wretched thing he is, as in the flesh, that his heart may be transferred to a new centre altogether. Nothing can be more distasteful to a spiritual mind than to hear people professedly giving a Christian testimony which begins and ends with themselves. However natural it may be to a newborn soul to talk of himself, it is a very disappointing feature in one who has professed to know the Lord for some time. It is for the effectual displacement of all this, and to transfer the heart to a new centre altogether, that the experience of which we are speaking is divinely necessary for our souls. God has to come in and detach us from that which is our natural centre, that He may link our affections with another Person—even with *Christ*—and make Him everything to our hearts, so that our association *with Him* may be known, and may become the deep, lasting joy of our souls. It is this that necessitates deliverance, and this is its blessed end.

In the eleven verses of Psalm 42 the words "I," "me," "my," occur thirty-five times, and six times the psalmist uses the expression "my soul." He is thoroughly *self-occupied*, but he is not *self-satisfied*—he is thirsting for God. Unhappy as such a condition may be, it is ten thousand times better than Laodicean complacency and self-satisfaction. The latter is what characterises Christendom today, and it is that which we ought to dread more than anything else. *Self-sufficiency* is a veil upon the heart, which blinds it to everything that is of God.

"Therefore will I remember Thee from the land of Jordan, and of the Hermonites, from the hill Mizar" (verse 6). The three places here mentioned are suggestive, to my mind, of three ways in which self is reduced to nothingness in the believer. (1) By inward exercise. (2) By the testings of the wilderness. (3) By special discipline from God. We may look briefly at each of the three.

(1) In the latter part of Romans 7 we find the experience of one who, through grace, delights in the law of God after the inward man, and is earnestly seeking to carry out God's holy will, but he finds a law in his members—a law of sin—to which he is in helpless captivity. He becomes painfully conscious that sin dwells in him, and eventually reaches the conclusion that in him, that is, in his flesh, there is nothing but sin—good he cannot find. It is by the law that he discovers this—by the effort to carry out God's will—so that which was ordained to life he finds to be unto death. *He is brought down to death.* Death is that state out of which nothing comes for God, and if I am truly conscious that good does not dwell in me I am brought down to death—the "land of Jordan." Paul reached this point in a very short time because he was in dead earnest. He learned in three days a lesson which it often takes a lifetime to learn. We are long on the road because we are so

little in earnest about it. But all this is inward experience and exercise. Outwardly Paul's life was most exemplary; it is not at all outward failure that others might see; it is the inward exercise in which the true character of sin in the flesh is discovered.

(2) The object of all the trial and testing of the wilderness was, as Deuteronomy 8: 2 tells us, "to humble thee, and to prove thee, to know what was in thine heart, whether thou wouldest keep His commandments, or no." God leads us by a trying and rugged path (Hermon means "rugged") that the naughtiness and pride of our hearts may be discovered. God loves us too well to allow us to be deceived as to our true character as in the flesh. He puts us in the very circumstances that bring it out. Not one of us can escape this testing and sifting. And as our true character is thus brought to light, we fret and chafe and murmur. How inexpressibly vexatious it is to always have something turning up that gives occasion to our hearts to show what is in them! If we only had a path in which we could always acquit ourselves creditably, how different it would be! If things would only go as we should like, how well and happily should we get on! Yes, and how supremely self-satisfied we should become! But God will find us out, and so He causes us to traverse this land of the Hermonites until our hearts in their bitterness say, 'Why does God put me into such circumstances as these? Why does He not make it easier for me? Why does something always occur to overturn my efforts to be good, and to make fruitless all my desires to be holy? If God would order things differently for me, my life would not be the contemptible failure that it now is.' Has you heart never uttered such language as this? Do you know what it means? Why, it is casting the blame of your sin upon God, and this is the outcome of satanic enmity. It is the bite of the serpent. In a thousand

ways you have proved the goodness and mercy of God, and yet your heart is capable of turning round upon Him and suggesting that His ordering for you is to blame for all your failure. What a discovery this is of those hidden springs of enmity against God that rise in the carnal mind!

(3) The "hill Mizar" (the little hill) may represent any special discipline of God by which we are made consciously weak and small. When Paul came down from the third heaven there was given him a thorn for the flesh, a messenger of Satan to buffet him; and this, he tells us, was "lest I should be exalted above measure." It was his "hill Mizar." God allowed Satan so to act on Paul's flesh, by some form of bodily suffering, that he was conscious of nothing in himself but weakness. You may say, 'That must be a miserable experience.' Well, Paul was not miserable; he was supremely happy. He says, 'Most gladly therefore will I rather glory in my weakness, that the power of Christ may tabernacle over me… I take pleasure in weakness… for when I am weak, then am I strong.' He was happy to have all his own strength reduced to nothingness, that he might prove instead the sufficiency of the Lord's grace and Christ's strength.

As to these three forms of self-reduction, the first two are *instructive*, while the third is rather *protective*. The inward exercise of Romans 7 and the testing of the wilderness serve the purpose of teaching us what sin in the flesh is, and what is in our hearts; while such special discipline of God as Paul's thorn is rather to protect us from the unaltered tendencies of the flesh. The latter is *always* needed, and goes on in one form or other to the end of our course here.

It is well for us to get to the end and the bottom of ourselves, for when we really get to the bottom with God we reach deliverance. Paul no sooner reaches

"O wretched man that I am! who shall deliver me out of this body of death?" than he exclaims, "I thank God, through Jesus Christ our Lord." The children of Israel, bitten by the serpent and brought down to death, found the way of life opened up by beholding the serpent of brass. When we truly abhor ourselves, we are prepared to rejoice in the blessed fact that our old man has been crucified with Christ—that sin in the flesh was condemned when Christ died, that our whole history as in the flesh closed before God in His death—and that this is our title to be free. I have now a righteous title to have done with myself because Christ has died. To prepare me for this I have to learn the necessity for death in my own experience, but *the death of Christ* is my title to be free. It is by the appropriation of His death that I reach liberty and life; that death has severed me from all that I was as in Adam. "I am crucified with Christ." I am free from myself, and free to have Christ before me, and to learn how I am associated with Him in new creation. In a word, I pass from the experience of Psalm 42 into that of Psalm 45.

The change is most striking. It is no longer "I," "me," "my," but "Thou," "Thee," "Thy." The soul has got a totally new Object and Centre; it has come to God's Centre. The old astronomers found the motions of the planetary bodies quite inexplicable because they looked upon the earth as the centre of the universe. It was not until a bold, free mind travelled forth into space and found a new centre that harmony and order were seen to reign where all had seemed confusion before. So long as the soul is self-centred it can make no real acquaintance with, or progress in, the thoughts and purposes of God. But when Christ gets His right place for our souls, we begin to apprehend the wondrous depth and perfection of those thoughts and purposes, and then our blessings are all, as it were, glorified. We are then able to leave self altogether behind, and to enter the atmosphere of divine love. Psalm 45 is called "a song of the Beloved"; and so completely has it this character, that there is not a word in it about what the Lord *has done*; the heart is engaged with *Himself*. *Love* thinks more of the Giver than His gifts—more of the love than of the work which love has wrought. It is when the Person of Christ is thus before the heart that it begins to bubble over, and to burn as did those of the disciples on the way to Emmaüs when the Stranger spoke of "the things concerning Himself." Then, verily, the heart is inditing a good matter; it is absorbed in the contemplation of the altogether lovely One. *Self* has been learned and given up as worthless, and another Person, who eclipses everything, is now before the soul. Four great and precious facts as to that Person come before the heart.

1. "Thou art fairer than the children of men." It is only the believer who can see attractiveness and beauty in Jesus. To the natural man Barabbas is more lovely than Jesus; not that he likes Barabbas to break into his house or pick his pocket, but he can understand Barabbas, and he cannot understand Jesus. The Beatitudes (Matt. 5: 3–10) give us the portrait of the One who is "fairer than the children of men." Poor in spirit, a Mourner in this world of sin and woe, meek, hungering and thirsting after righteousness, merciful, pure in heart, a Peacemaker, One persecuted for righteousness' sake—these are the traits of His beauty. The natural man says, 'These are poor things, and but of plain appearance. A man of such a character as that is no good in this world.' The man who will not assert himself because he feels that God has no place here, who will bear injury and wrong without murmuring, whose one insatiable desire is to do the will of God, though it entails nothing but suffering and

persecution here, is looked upon by the world with contempt, and where the conscience has felt the power of his testimony, he is positively hated. "He is despised and rejected of men." Christ was just the opposite to the world's ideal man. A man who by brilliant genius, commanding personality, and indomitable perseverance has secured position, wealth, or fame, is the world's ideal. The one who makes himself great in the eyes of men is the world's hero, and I fear that Christians are often deceived by the glitter of fame and the acclamations of human applause, and they come to admire men who are the very opposite to the meek and lowly Jesus. Oh that we may be kept in the secret of God's presence, so as to know what *He* appreciates in man! It is a proof of immense favour from God if in our heart's estimation Christ is "fairer than the children of men." It is easy to sing hymns, and to use the most precious expressions in Scripture in a sentimental way, but it is another thing for our hearts really to find rest and satisfaction in the moral perfections of Christ. It is blessed to find the heart thrilling with something of the ecstasy which the Bride feels as she describes Him—beginning with "The chiefest among ten thousand," and ending with "He is altogether lovely" (Song of Solomon 5: 10–16).

2. "Grace is poured into Thy lips." There has been One here in whom and by whom all the grace of God could express itself. The Son of God took a place of perfect dependence here as the Vessel of that grace, and in that dependent place the Lord God gave Him the tongue of the Learner, that He should know how to speak a word in season to him that is weary (Isaiah 50: 4). Well might the Nazarenes marvel at the gracious words which proceeded out of His mouth. Well might those sent to take Him have to confess, "Never man spake like this man." The evangelist Luke presents Him specially in the

blessed character of the Minister of grace, and how full and matchless is the record! The synagogues at Nazareth and Capernaum, the sea-shore of Galilee, the house of Levi, the corn-fields, the gate of the city of Nain, the Pharisee's house, and all the scenes of that holy ministry right on to Calvary, have their own sweet tale to tell of the grace that was poured into His lips, and which flowed forth from those lips in a fulness which nothing could stay. Nay, the very cavils and opposition of unbelief and self-righteousness only served to bring it out more fully, as the attempt to stay the flow of some mighty river might cause it to overflow all its banks. The *grace of God* has told itself out here in a Man. God has found the satisfaction of His heart in having One here who not only could, and did, fill the whole compass of man's responsibility with perfection, but was the full expression of divine grace here, and this, withal, in perfect dependence. There was but one Person who could thus bring and express the grace of God in a world of sin, and He has done it perfectly. Blessed for ever be His sacred Name!

3. The "sword" and the "arrows" (verses 3, 5) bear witness that the One into whose lips grace was poured has been rejected here. Judgment awaits His enemies—judgment rendered inevitable by the fact that men have refused the grace of God, and rejected the One in whom it all came. This world has rewarded Christ evil for good, and hatred for His love. It is now the scene of His rejection—soon to be the scene of victorious judgment whereby God shall make His foes His footstool. But for the present Christ is dishonoured and disinherited here. He has been cut off and had nothing. He is cast aside as worthless by men, who see no beauty in Him that they should desire Him.

4. But in wondrous contrast to this we read, "therefore God hath blessed Thee for ever" (verse 2).

Every step of that pathway of lowly and devoted love has had its answer. Not *here*, indeed, for that Blessed One had nothing here; none of this world's honour graced His brow; its commonest civilities were denied Him; He had not where to lay His head; nor, so far as we know, did He ever possess a penny. *His blessing is in another sphere*; His exaltation is in heaven; He is crowned with glory and honour at the right hand of God. He is the Man of joy for ever now, for He has entered the fulness of joy in the presence of God, and the pleasures for evermore which are at His right hand. "Thou hast made Him most blessed for ever: Thou hast made Him exceeding glad with Thy countenance" (Psalm 21: 6). I referred a few moments ago to the Beatitudes as giving the portrait of the One fairer than the children of men, and I may now call your attention to a verse which follows them: 'Rejoice, and be exceeding glad: for great is your reward *in heaven*' (Matt. 5: 12). The Beatitudes have their fruition in heaven: Christ has His blessings, His reward and compensation, there. Everything was unsuited to Him here, but He is now in a scene where everything is suited to Him. Can we not truly say

> "O Lord, 'tis joy to look above,
> And see Thee on the throne"?

We are still in the place of His rejection, but we joy in His exaltation *there*; and, through infinite grace, *we are linked with Him* in the place of His joy and His glory. What could be more wonderful and blessed?

'God, thy God, hath anointed Thee with the oil of gladness *above Thy fellows*' (verse 7). Here the marvellous fact is disclosed that Christ in glory has "fellows"—companions. Upon earth He was *alone* in His beauty—the single Corn of wheat. There could be no link between the Second Man out of heaven and the sinful race of Adam. But in His death the whole race for whom He died was condemned and set aside in judgment, and as the risen and glorified One He has become the Head of a new race, to whom He has given eternal life, and who are associated with Him in His wondrous place as Man before God and the Father. By the will of God we are "sanctified" through the offering of the body of Jesus Christ once (Heb. 10: 10). That is, by His death we have been set apart from everything that we were as in the flesh, that we might be *of Him* in new creation—all of one with Himself—His fellows. "For both He that sanctifieth and they who are sanctified are all of one: for which cause He is not ashamed to call them brethren" (Heb. 2: 11). Beloved brethren, does not this captivate and satisfy the heart? To see that by the death of Christ I am entitled to be free from myself—to drop everything that I am as in the flesh—that I may pass into conscious association with that blessed One in glory. Now, indeed, my heart has got a new centre, and has begun to learn with God the greatness of the thoughts of divine love. I begin to realise the immensity of God's purpose and grace, and to be lost in wonder, love, and praise. Thus we learn the character and dignity of the priestly company of whom Christ can speak as "My brethren," and to whom He can declare the Father's Name. For if we learn these precious things, as we must learn everything, *individually*, it is that we may know the character of the *company* to which, through grace, we belong.

Notice, too, that it is in connection with this we have the Holy Ghost mentioned. 'God, thy God, hath anointed Thee *with the oil of gladness* above Thy fellows.' The gift of the Spirit is distinctly connected with the fact that Jesus is glorified (John 7: 39). It is with *Christ in glory* that the Holy Ghost links us. As the glorified Man He has received the Holy Ghost (Acts 2: 33), and this anointing He shares with His brethren. As Aaron and his sons were all sprinkled with the same "anointing oil" in the day of their consecration (Exodus 29: 21), so Christ and His "brethren" have this blessed anointing in common. Yet in this, as in everything else, He must have the pre-eminence; He is anointed "above" His fellows, and our faith and love rejoice that it should be so.

Then observe the peculiar character in which the Holy Ghost is here spoken of—"the oil of gladness." In the New Testament we find again and again that *joy* is connected with the Holy Ghost. "The disciples were filled with joy, and with the Holy Ghost" (Acts 13: 52). "Joy in the Holy Ghost" (Rom. 14: 17). (Compare also Eph. 5: 18, 19.) Does not this throw a glorious light upon the character of the Christian's joys? The Holy Ghost is the divine power by which our hearts are brought into conscious association with Christ; He is the 'well of living water springing up into everlasting life' (John 4: 14). His indwelling gives capacity to taste of heavenly joys, the joys of that ineffable scene of divine affections into which Christ has entered as 'the Father's glorified.' Do we not long to taste of those joys? Are we prepared to go in for them? Do we really believe that the Holy Ghost dwells in us to make our hearts *overflow* with heavenly gladness?

The effect of gladness within is fragrance without. "All thy garments smell of myrrh, and aloes, and cassia, out of the ivory palaces, whereby they have made thee glad" (verse 8). The fragrance I take to be the fruit of the Spirit—the qualities, graces, and moral perfections of Christ—"love, joy, peace, longsuffering, gentleness, goodness, faith, meekness, temperance" (Gal. 5: 22). I have no doubt we should all like to be thus fragrant, but I am quite sure that this will only be the case as we are in the gladness of which I have spoken. It is not the clearness and accuracy of our scriptural intelligence, or the ability with which we can present the truth, that impresses people so much as the fact that they can discern when we have an inward satisfaction and gladness to which they are strangers. I well remember hearing a beloved servant of the Lord speak of the knowledge of Christ in glory. I was greatly impressed, but it was not so much by the information imparted as by the conviction, 'That man has something which I should like to have.' If others can see that we have something which they have not, it will set them thirsting to have it too. Nothing helps people so much as this, and they can soon discover when we have this heavenly "gladness" in our souls. If there is the gladness within there is sure to be the fragrance without.

May each of us prove the blessed reality of all this, so that instead of thirsting we may be satisfied and overflowing.

LOVED UNTO THE END

John 13: 1–17

I have read these verses with a desire that the Lord may awaken us to the reality and greatness of the thoughts of divine love. Nothing can be sweeter than to repose in that love when it is known, and the heart is free to rest in it. The soul may have a long journey to reach it experimentally; there may be many needs and exercises to be met and removed on the way; self and the world may have to be learned; but the great end of all our exercises—and, I may add, of all our deliverances is that we rest in the thoughts of divine love, and that love becomes in a very real way the portion of our hearts. If our hearts are not in the circle of divine love they have really got *nothing*, for as Christians we have no portion on earth or in the world; our portion is in divine love. Thank God! it is a blessed and a satisfying portion.

The disciples had left all and followed Jesus with the kingdom in prospect. They looked for righteousness to be established here, and were much occupied with the thought of how *they* would stand in the new order of things—disputing who should be the greatest, and so on. But instead of righteousness being established here, the Righteous One was rejected; the Lord was crucified. As to this world the disciples had lost everything and gained nothing, but to compensate for this they got divine love. Many are content to have assurance of pardon and eternal security, without forsaking all to follow a rejected Christ; that is, they have not in heart and spirit broken with the world, and they do not know what it is to have a portion in divine love.

I should like, in the first place, to bring before your hearts the statement of verse 3. "Jesus knowing… that He was come from God, and went to God." How much is conveyed in these simple words! What infinite and amazing facts are involved in this brief and pregnant sentence! Jesus came *from God* into a world of sin, of man's ruin, of Satan's triumph, and of God's grief and dishonour; and He has secured everything *for God*, so that He could go back *to God* as the One who has removed every hindrance to the full display and triumph of divine love. We must not expect to find that the work of the Lord Jesus is looked at in this Gospel from the sinner's standpoint. That which will meet the need of a sinner's conscience must be sought elsewhere. But, beloved brethren, let us not deprive our hearts of the deepest and richest spiritual joys by thinking only of the death of the Lord Jesus as that which meets the dire necessity of our souls. Let us seek to enter into what that death was for God, and into the wondrous blessings of divine love for which it opens the way according to the counsel and purpose of the heart of

God. The work of Christ is infinitely great in moral grandeur as the everlasting basis on which the purposes of divine love are secured, and it is from this point of view that it is presented to us in John's gospel. Let us turn to five Scriptures which bring before us some of the things that have been secured for the satisfaction of divine love.

1. "Behold the Lamb of God, which taketh away the sin of the world" (John 1: 29). In the beginning God created the heavens and the earth for His own pleasure, and pronounced them very good; but sin came in and deprived God of satisfaction in His created universe, and no reparation was, or could be, made until Jesus came as the Lamb of God to take up the whole question of sin, and to maintain all that was due to divine majesty and holiness in connection therewith; so that God, being perfectly glorified as to it, might be free to set up a "new heaven and a new earth"—a universe of perfect bliss where no trace of sin or its effects can ever come. The created universe of Genesis 1 will be cleared of sin, and brought into perfect suitability to God. The Fulness of the Godhead will reconcile all things to itself, "whether they be things in earth, or things in heaven" (Col. 1: 20). And all this will be established on the everlasting basis that God has been glorified in respect of sin, and that basis will ensure its eternal stability. Here, then, at the outset we obtain a view of things too vast to comprehend. The magnitude and scope of it are beyond us, but surely the feeblest heart will rejoice to know that a world of bliss has been secured for God—a world where divine love will have eternal satisfaction and rest—all secured by Jesus, who will be the Centre and Sun of that universe of bliss.

2. "I am the Good Shepherd: the Good Shepherd giveth His life for the sheep... My sheep hear My voice, and I know them, and they follow me: and I

give unto them eternal life; and they shall never perish, neither shall any pluck them out of My hand. My Father, which gave them Me, is greater than all; and no man is able to pluck them out of My Father's hand. I and My Father are one" (John 10: 11, 27–30). For some years I thought that John 10 was written to make the believer sure that eternal blessing was secured *to him*. I rejoice to know that it does this, but there is far more in it than this. The Good Shepherd laid down His life for the sheep that He might have the joy of securing them *for Himself and for the Father*. The Father and the Son wanted the sheep for themselves, and the death of Christ is the righteous title of divine love to take possession, and to keep possession, of them. The Father and the Son wanted a company whom they might introduce to the circle of divine love, with a nature suitable to that circle, and capable of appreciating and responding to it. The right to have such a company has been secured to God by Jesus, and none of those who compose it will ever be lost. God set up man in innocence on the ground of responsibility, and lost him. But the sheep are held on the ground of redemption, they are partakers of the divine nature, and they are secured for the satisfaction of divine love. No one can question the right of the Father and the Son to have and to hold the sheep; and if we see what it has cost the Father and the Son to secure us, it cannot fail to give us the most blessed assurance. Much may yet have to be done for us. We shall need support, preservation, discipline. If we are left here a little longer we shall need the grace, mercy, and forbearance of God in a thousand ways, but all that will be needed in the future to keep us for the Father and the Son is small compared with the stupendous cost at which divine love secured us. 'Hereby perceive we love, because He laid down His life for us' (1 John 3: 16).

3. “He prophesied that Jesus should die for that nation; and not for that nation only, but that also He should gather together in one the children of God that were scattered abroad” (John 11: 51, 52). In the company secured by divine love there can be no fleshly distinctions. It is a company in the unity of the divine nature—“one flock.” Hence the Lord prays, “That they all may be one; as Thou, Father, art in Me, and I in Thee, that they also may be one in Us: that the world may believe that Thou hast sent Me” (John 17: 21). The present thought of God is to have a company in the unity of the divine nature. In that company “There is neither Jew nor Greek”—no religious distinctions; “neither bond nor free”—no social distinctions; “neither male nor female”—no natural distinctions; but “ye are all one in Christ Jesus” (Gal. 3: 28).

4. “Verily, verily, I say unto you, Except a corn of wheat fall into the ground and die, it abideth alone: but if it die, it bringeth forth much fruit” (John 12: 24). The “flock” of chapter 10, and “the children of God” of chapter 11, are evidently the same company. Now we get the additional fact presented that those who compose this company are *of Christ’s order*. He has gone into death that He might become the Parent-grain of this company. He bears fruit after His kind. His death is the end of all that we were as children of Adam, that we might be in association with Him as the Risen One—His brethren—“all of one” with Himself, and introduced by Him to His own position and relationship with His God and Father.

5. “The only-begotten Son, who is in the bosom of the Father, *He* hath declared Him” (John 1: 18). “He that hath seen Me hath seen the Father” (John 14: 9). Thus far I have spoken of His death, but it is important to remember that He did not go back to God without having first perfectly revealed the Father. By doing so He exposed the true character of the world, as we read, “now have they both seen and

hated both Me and My Father" (John 15: 24). On the other hand, He brought the perfect revelation of the Father to those who, by divine grace, could appreciate that revelation. But think what an infinite satisfaction it was for God to have One here who could fully reveal Him. The Father delights to be appreciated, and in order to do this He must be revealed, and Jesus has revealed Him. He must have been equal with the Father to do so. Even in human things I could not give perfect expression to a person's mind and character if I was not equal to that person. Keeping this in mind it is very blessed to see *how* He revealed the Father. It was by never speaking a word or doing an act of His own will. His words were the Father's words, and the Father that dwelt in Him, He did the works. In that lowly, obedient One the Father was perfectly revealed. Every thought of the Father's heart was perfectly expressed in Him.

Now in chapter 13 everything is looked at as secured. Jesus came *from God* alone, but He has gone *to God* as the Head of a new and blessed race, and as the One who has secured everything *for God*. He is the perfect contrast to Adam the first, who came from God, and lost everything, and went to the dust. The Last Adam came from God, secured everything *for God*, and has gone *to God* as the glorified Head of a new race brought into divine love in association with Himself, and Head of a new creation in which all the thoughts of that love will be effected and displayed for ever. For the Father has "given all things into His hand." Think of the greatness of it. Jesus stepped into the midst of all the ruin and moral chaos which sin had caused, and so secured everything for God that the Father has given *all things* into His hand. He has acquired, may we say, the right to be Head of the new creation—to be the Centre and Sun of that universe of bliss which He has secured for God, and which He will fill with divine glory. Those far-reaching realms of light and glory are fitly inherited by Him who has put them all in suitability to divine love. In such a circle our souls are lost, dazzled, bewildered. The expanse of divine glory is too great for us. We cannot comprehend *divine greatness;* thank God! the portion of our hearts is *divine love*.

Nothing can be of greater importance for our hearts than to apprehend the meaning of the words, "Jesus knew that His hour was come that He should depart out of this world unto the Father" (John 13: 1). His coming into the world has secured everything for God, and has brought the perfect revelation of the Father into it, but it has also proved in the fullest way the true character of the world. It is a scene of darkness, hatred, and dishonour to God. The fact that the Son of the Father has been here has demonstrated that there is nothing in the world for the Father. So that He could say, "Now is the judgment of this world" (John 12: 31), and again the Holy Ghost convicts the world "of judgment, because the prince of this world is judged" (John 16: 11). The character of the prince of this world is fully revealed, and in that revelation the whole system of which he is the head is fully exposed. The world is controlled by, and derives its character from, one who hates the Father and the Son. There is no place in the world for the Father or the Son. This has been fully proved; so that the world is not at all in the experimental stage so far as God is concerned. It is so with men; they are trying to improve it, and to see what they can make of it. But for God the world is a judged thing; it has been tried, proved, and fully exposed. The whole truth as to it is out. Some people say the world is getting better, and others say it is getting worse. They are both wrong. It is no better than when the Son of God was here, and it could not possibly be worse. Jesus has left it because there was nothing in it for the Father; He has left it as a scene fully exposed and judged. Many believers have not accepted this; they think the world can be improved; their hearts have not apprehended the immense fact that Jesus has left this world as a judged thing, and has gone to the Father. The result is they do not enter into the precious things revealed in John 13–17. If the world is not a judged thing for our hearts I am sure we shall never understand these chapters.

But if the blessed Lord has no link with the world, He has a most intimate and precious link with a certain company in the world—the "flock" of chapter 10; the "children of God" of chapter 11; the "much fruit" of chapter 12—now spoken of as '*His own which were in the world*.' His heart is bound to that company in inconceivable love; it is His peculiar treasure—the "pearl of great price" to obtain which 'he sold all that he had' (Matt. 13: 46). Indeed, the consideration of all that is involved in being "His own" would carry our hearts over the whole range of divine grace, and would lead us in a wonderful way into the thoughts of divine love. The saints are *His own by the Father's gift*. "Thine they were," says the Son, "and Thou gavest them Me" (John 17: 6). Before time began the Father took possession of us by making us the subjects of His gracious thought and counsel, and His purpose and object in thus taking possession of us was that He might give us to the Son. In the thoughts of divine love we are of such value as to be a suitable gift from the Father to the Son—a gift worthy of the Giver and the Receiver. We shall be for ever the expression to the Son of the Father's love to Him. This is beyond our comprehension, but is it not precious to think of?

His own by His choice of us. "I have chosen you out of the world" (John 15: 19). When He was here He called to Him whom He would. It was no indiscriminate or haphazard company that gathered round Him, brought together by chance of circumstance or by the decision of human will. It was a called and chosen company, and it is just as true, beloved brethren, that He has chosen *us*. He wants us for Himself; He must have us; now He has got us; we are *His own*.

His own by redemption. "I am the Good Shepherd: the Good Shepherd giveth His life for the sheep" (John 10: 11). He has an indisputable right to us, for He has redeemed us, and in doing so has proved that His love was "strong as death." He could only secure us for Himself at the cost of His life, and He has given "his life for the sheep." There can never be such an *expression* of His love again, but the *love* that thus expressed itself remains unchanged.

His own by moral conformity to Himself. "They are not of the world, even as I am not of the world" (John 17: 16). The world is made up of "the lust of the flesh, and the lust of the eyes, and the pride of life" (1 John 2: 16). In perfect contrast to this there was divine love, divine light, and divine lowliness in Him. He was not of the world. And as we are formed in, and grow up in, the divine nature these same things will characterise us who are "His own."

His own in the affection of our hearts. "The two disciples heard Him speak, and they followed Jesus" (John 1: 37). He had not said a word to them yet, but the raptured gaze of the Baptist had rested upon Him, and the delight of his heart had expressed itself in the involuntary exclamation, "Behold the Lamb of God." And in simple, spontaneous affection the two went after Him—*His own* in their affections. Again, Peter as the spokesman of the twelve says in a moment of testing, "Lord, to whom shall we go? thou hast the words of eternal life" (John 6: 68). He had made Himself indispensable to their hearts—He was unrivalled in their affections. There was something about them which made them precious to the Father—"The Father Himself loveth you, because ye have loved Me" (John 16: 27). May God give us hearts like theirs!

His own to be loved by Him. "As the Father hath loved me, so have I loved you" (John 15: 9). Could anything equal this? Does it not fill the heart with unspeakable satisfaction and joy? Nothing can measure this love; no sounding-line can fathom it. If we had, like Paul, "suffered the loss of all things" here, would not His love be a sufficient compensation? Rebecca lost her own country, but she got Isaac's love. The servant could speak of "flocks, and herds, and silver, and gold, and menservants, and maidservants, and camels, and asses" (Genesis 24: 35), but you may depend upon it that Isaac's love was the great thing to Rebecca. We are often occupied with our blessings, but the great thing is *the love of Christ*. And this love never fails. "Having loved His own which were in the world, He loved them unto the end."

We must understand the character of the company and the character of the world in order to apprehend the meaning of John 13. It would be a natural thing for such a company to go out of the world, as Jesus was about to do, for "His own" are in the circle of divine love, and there is nothing in the world that answers to that love. "The world knoweth us not, because it knew Him not" (1 John 3: 1). The world was so unsuited to Him that He must needs leave it and go to the Father, yet He leaves His own in it. So that there is a company suited to divine affections and brought into the circle of those affections, and yet left "in the world." This is the position of "His own" at the present moment. Left in the world, and yet within the circle of divine love; that is, belonging to the very circle into which Jesus has gone. He has gone to the Father; He has returned to that blessed circle of divine affections where all is suited to Him; but He has not left His own outside the circle of those affections. That circle touches the earth and holds within itself "His own" which are in the world. As to divine affections, Jesus is not in one circle and His own in another. The circle of divine and heavenly affections where the Son is with the Father touches the earth, and includes His own which are in the world. It is a circle of heavenly love, but we come within it even here.

This peculiar and blessed fact must be apprehended if we wish to understand this chapter. That is, we are within the circle of divine affections, but not yet taken out of the place where there is nothing for the Father or the Son. If we were *altogether* in the circle of divine affections, divine love could *rest* in our undisturbed blessing. But we are still in a scene, and in a condition, where there are innumerable elements at work which are of a nature contrary to those affections. And therefore so long as we are in the world divine love cannot *rest*; that love must needs consider all these contrary and hindering elements, and must *serve* in its solicitude to maintain us in the enjoyment of, and in suitability to, that heavenly circle to which we belong. Hence the service of Jesus—so beautifully and touchingly presented to us in figure in this chapter.

Divine love considers everything—knows what the world is—knows what we are—and loves to the end. It is an out-and-out love—love in spite of everything. You may say, 'I find so many things to hinder.' Do you think you have found something the Lord overlooked? No! the Lord sees all, and knows all, and *loves to the end*. Nothing can turn that love. It was the darkest moment for the blessed Lord; He was just about to suffer; the dark clouds of that dreaded "hour" were closing in upon Him; and yet He rose from supper and girded Himself to wash their feet. He was thinking not of Himself but of them. On the other hand, it is as "knowing that the Father had given all things into His hands, and that He was come from God, and went to God," that He rises and girds Himself for His service of love. The greatness and glory of which He was so perfectly conscious give an inexpressible depth of meaning to this unique act of divine love. Their condition, too, perfectly known by Him, did not stay that love. He knew that one would deny Him, and all forsake Him—the treachery of Judas and the weakness of Peter were alike before Him—but His love retired, if we may so say, into itself, and acted altogether from itself. "He riseth from supper, and laid aside His garments; and took a towel, and girded Himself. After that He poureth water into a bason, and began to wash the disciples' feet, and to wipe them with the towel wherewith He was girded."

That it was a service with an unknown meaning at the time we may gather from the Lord's words to Peter. "What I do thou knowest not now; but thou shalt know hereafter." This shows it was much more than an object lesson in humanity; for if that had been its chief intent the force of it was never so apparent as at the moment. We are constrained to look for a wider meaning and a deeper significance than this in the action of the Lord. And, indeed, He gives us the key to it when, in answer to Peter's objection, He says, 'If I wash thee not, thou hast no *part with Me*.' Solemn and impressive words. May their force and meaning come home to our hearts with divine power.

I must again remind you of the fact that, although we belong to the circle of divine love, we are still "in the world." The Lord is altogether in the circle of divine love—He has gone to the Father—and as our hearts enter into that circle we have *part with Him*. But here is another solemn disclosure of the nature of the world, and of the true character of all its influences; a solemn warning, too, as to our susceptibility to those influences, and as to the condition in which we remain while "in the world." We are entitled to be in the circle of divine love; divine grace has called us into it; and as being partakers of the divine nature we are of that circle; we are of it as belonging to the Father and the Son; and yet it is not less true that the blessed Lord says to each one of us, 'If I wash thee not, thou hast *no part with Me*.' There is an absolute necessity for this service of love to maintain our hearts in freedom from the influences of the world, and in such superiority to all that is incidental to our present condition, that in heart and spirit we may really enter the circle of divine affections, and have part with Him who has gone to the Father. We are in a condition that renders this service necessary. There is that in us to which the dust of the world sticks, if I may be allowed to express it thus simply. In the case of our blessed Lord there was nothing to which the dust of the world could adhere. He was altogether the Holy One of God, and all the influences and tendencies of this world were repelled from Him by the absolute holiness and purity of His Person. There was no moral point of contact between Him and the world, though He passed through it in lowly and perfect grace. We are not only in the world as to our bodily condition, but there is that in us which affords a point of moral contact with the world. There is that in us to which the dust of the world can adhere. Our blessed Lord did not need to have His feet washed, but we do. Our condition renders us susceptible to the influences of the world. It is not that we sin, but we are affected by things here; they have a tendency to occupy our hearts, and to influence us in such a way that we are taken out of the enjoyment of that circle of divine affections into which Jesus has gone, and to which, through infinite grace, we belong. So far from the defilement of John 13 being actual failure or sin, I believe the most spiritual person is the one who will appreciate this service of love—he is the one who will have the deepest sense of the need of having his feet washed. It would be a sad thing to suppose—and certainly Scripture does not assert—that there is absolute necessity for a believer to commit sin. But there is absolute *necessity* for the feet-washing in order to have part with Christ, and hence the defilement which that washing removes must be a necessity too. It is that which is unavoidable so long as we are "in the world."

But let us follow the instruction of the chapter a little further. Peter, looking upon the scene in a natural way, had first of all refused to allow the Lord to wash his feet; but on hearing that the washing was with a view to having part with Him, he exclaims with his usual fervency of spirit, "Lord, not my feet only, but also my hands and my head." This gives occasion to the Lord to make the important statement of verse 10, "He that is washed [bathed] needeth not save to wash his feet, but is clean every whit." It is evident that the figure used is that of a person who has bathed, and in walking from the bath has defiled his feet with the dust of the floor. He does not need to return to the bath; he only requires that his feet should be washed, to be "clean every whit."

Let us seek, in the first place, to understand what is meant by "he that is washed." It has sometimes been taken as the cleansing of the blood, but this has no warrant in the Scripture. It is expressly cleansing *by water*, and where we find this in Scripture it seems to me to be a figure of passing into a wholly new order of things, and of being made suitable for it. The priests were washed in the day of their consecration. (Exodus 29: 4.) It was a ceremony indicative of the fact that they were set apart for this special service; it was their introduction to a new order of life; and was expressive of the fact that they were introduced to it in a way that rendered them suitable for it. Scripture speaks of the "washing of regeneration" (Titus 3: 5), where the thought is evidently that of introduction to a totally new order of things; and Paul says to the Corinthians, "ye are washed"—enforcing thereby the fact that they had been brought out of everything that constituted their former life. Now, how had the disciples been "washed"? May we not learn something as to it from John 15: 3? 'Now ye are clean *through the word which I have spoken unto you*.' The word of Christ had wrought in power in their hearts, and they had been introduced by it to an entirely new order of things. No doubt the new birth is essential to this, and the "washing" involves the thought of the death of Christ; and is, so to speak, the application of His death as that which separates us from the world and from ourselves as in the flesh; but it evidently includes the knowledge of Christ by His word. 'Ye are clean *through the word which I have spoken unto you*.' Christ had *made Himself known*, by His word, in the hearts of the disciples. His word expressed *Himself*, and the knowledge of Himself had freed their hearts from everything that was of the world. It was a great thing for a few fishermen to be found in complete superiority to all the political, social, and religious influences that were around them. They were delivered from the whole current of things and opinions that prevailed in the world. They were brought outside it all—morally purified from it all—by the knowledge of Christ. "To whom shall we go? Thou hast the words of eternal life," are words which express the heart-feelings of the company thus "washed" and "clean." They had, if I may so say, the moral cleansing of a new object. The knowledge of that blessed Person had delivered them from the thoughts of men, and from the motives and principles of the world. The 'expulsive power' of the knowledge of Christ had displaced other things, and by the knowledge of Him they entered into an entirely new world. They were "washed."

"He that is washed needeth not save to wash his feet." The cleansing of the whole moral being, in the way of which I have spoken, is a divine operation that is never repeated, but there is continual need for the feet to be washed. It is the point of contact with this present scene which is the point of danger, and we cannot avoid this so long as we are in the world. The very thought of this may well move our affections deeply when we consider that it necessitates the untiring and devoted service of the One who loves "unto the end." It furnishes Him with opportunity to give continual expression to His love. But for this ministry of divine love our contact with the world, and our susceptibility to the influences of this present scene, would have the effect of permanently withdrawing our hearts from *part with Christ* in the circle of divine affections. Little do we know how the blessed Lord longs to have our hearts in company with Himself in that wondrous circle. May He be graciously pleased to draw us near to Himself, and give our hearts a deeper sense of His love.

The question may be asked, '*How* does the Lord wash our feet?' I cannot say much about it, but it seems to me that the washing of the feet partakes of the same nature as the washing all over. It is of the same character, though with a more limited range according to the present need. I believe our feet are washed by a fresh presentation of Christ to our affections. He brings Himself and His love before our hearts, and thus He displaces the dust of the world. It is a distinct service—the special service of His love while we are in the world. If our hearts are really touched by this I am sure we shall count more upon the Lord for His service, and we shall look more to Him for it. No doubt this service of love is for all "His own," but we ought to be exercised as to whether we have been in a condition to get the good of it. One must be consciously of "His own," and have the world as a judged thing, before he can realise the good of this precious service of divine love. There must also be a response—a looking for the service. I am afraid we are often like Peter; we will not allow the Lord to wash our feet. We give Him no opportunity of doing so. Do we not often read the Word and pray without turning *to the Lord* for His present and personal ministry of love?

Christ loves His own which are in the world, and He washes their feet. If we have part with Him we shall love His own, and we shall wash their feet. Those who taste the joys of that circle of divine affections cannot help longing that others should have their feet cleansed from the dust of the world, that they might enjoy their true portion according to the thoughts of divine love. It is as our own feet are washed that we become instrumental in washing the feet of our brethren. If my feet are not washed my heart is more or less under the power and influence of things here, and if I speak of these things I put a little more dust on my brother's feet. But if my feet have been washed the love of Christ and of the Father are known in my heart—I am in the circle of divine affections—and I naturally speak of the things that are in that circle. If I am enabled to bring these things before my brother's heart I wash his feet. It is not by telling him of his faults that I wash his feet. If he has sinned, or been overtaken in a fault, I must go to other Scriptures to know how to treat him. This chapter does not suppose any actual sin or fault, though I am convinced that if our feet are not washed we are in the greatest danger of falling into sin; if the dust accumulates on our feet it will undoubtedly result in sin. We must know the thoughts of divine love to understand this precious service of Christ; and I shall be thankful if the Lord uses His word tonight to lead us a little more into those thoughts.

THE DIVINE EFFECT OF THE TRUTH

John 1: 35–39; **20:** 17–20

Just one thought is upon my mind in connection with these Scriptures—the great importance of being divinely affected by the truth. If the truth does not form and move us it shows that we are only taking it up in the letter. There is not much advantage in this, for a man who has the letter of truth without its spirit is offensive to God. I admit that this is a solemn assertion, but it is nevertheless a true one. The pharisee and the lawyer are more repugnant to God than the publican and the sinner. The Pharisee and the lawyer are men well up in the externals and shell of the truth, but entirely unaffected by its kernel and spirit. The divine effect of truth is to mould and to move men.

In John 1 the blessed Lord is presented as the Lamb of God to the two disciples. The Lamb of God is a sacrificial title; it presents One to our hearts who comes from God to go into death, to bring the blessed testimony of what God is into the very place of sin and death. I have a strong impression that when Satan introduced sin into the world his object was not so much to destroy man as to introduce a state of things which should render it impossible for God to be known save as a righteous Judge. Satan's object is to keep the knowledge of God out of the heart of man, and thus to perpetuate that state of sin which was brought about in the first place by man giving ear to his slanderous insinuations. But what an answer God has given to all this! The very thing that seemed to make it impossible for Him to be known by man has furnished Him with an opportunity to make Himself known in all the blessedness of His nature. He has come out to reveal Himself in supreme and sovereign love in the very place of sin and death. Hence the "only-begotten Son, who is in the bosom of the Father"—the One who declares God perfectly—must needs be "the Lamb of God." There is necessity for Him to wear that sacrificial title, for He came to bring the testimony of divine love into DEATH.

In the very fact that the Son of God is invested with such a title is the pledge of the entire removal of sin, and thus of the total destruction of the works of the devil in the heart of man. Everyone who is in the light of this blessed fact, that the Son of God has assumed the title of Lamb of God, must be conscious that by His doing so a divine solution of the whole question of sin was absolutely ensured, and this in the way of divine love. The very fact that He was manifested here in that character rendered the whole thing absolutely secure because of the greatness of the One who was thus manifested.

Beloved brethren, how much have we been affected by the presentation to our hearts of the Lamb of God? We are in the light of the blessed revelation of Himself; divine love has been presented to us in its supremacy and sovereignty in the fact that He has gone into death. To what extent has the truth had its divine effect upon us?

The two disciples were greatly affected by the presentation to them of the Lamb of God. They left everything to follow Him. John the baptist was a great servant of God, but his ministry was in connection with the present order of things, in connection with an order of things where sin was. There was no solution of the question of sin, and therefore no full revelation of God presented in connection with John the baptist. But the "Lamb of God" was One who could solve the whole question of sin, and remove that question out of the way altogether, so as to be able to lead men into an entirely new order of things, where everything should be characterised by the knowledge of God according to the blessedness of the revelation in which He has come out in His only-begotten Son.

I do not say that the two disciples entered intelligently into all this at the time, but it is surely this which the Spirit of God would have us to gather from the lovely picture which He presents to us here. They followed Him to know where He dwelt, and it was everything to them to abide with Him. In figure they had left the circle of things where sin was, and they were in a new circle, where the perfect revelation of God was found, and where they could be in association with the One who was "with the Father." This is the divine effect of truth. It moved these disciples entirely out of the circle where sin was into all the blessed light of God, and into the company of Him who dwelt in the bosom of the Father.

If the Lamb of God is really before our hearts we shall be drawn away from all the pride and glory of this world, for we shall recognise it as the place of sin. But at the same time we shall be in the presence of divine love that could go even unto death to remove sin, and to reveal itself to our hearts. The divine effect of this would be to move our hearts entirely out of the present order of things. We should follow the Lamb of God through death into His own circle, where there is no trace of sin, where there is nothing to dim the shining of 'love supreme and bright.' The Lamb of God has passed into a scene where divine affections are in cloudless repose; He dwells in those affections, and He has accomplished in death the removal of sin so that we might enter that scene in association with Him for ever. He says, "Come and see"; He would have us to know the place of His abode, and if we miss this we miss the very kernel of Christianity—the crowning privilege and blessing of divine love. The whole work of grace in our souls, the Father's activity in sovereign love, the drawings of His gracious power, are all with a view to our introduction to this blessed association with His Son.

In John 20 everything that was involved in the title "Lamb of God" had been accomplished, and we find a company outside everything here—a company affected and brought together by the truth. The Risen One had said, "go to My brethren, and say unto them, I ascend unto My Father, and your Father; and to My God, and your God." The whole question of sin was disposed of, and consequent upon this THE TRUTH could be fully declared. And if, on the one hand, God and the Father was perfectly revealed, on the other there was a company secured to be in the blessed light of that revelation in association with the Son of God. The divine effect of this—and this is THE TRUTH—must be to put souls outside everything that is of man, and of the present order of things. In the upper room, with the doors shut to exclude the religious man after the flesh, the disciples had the company of Christ. The truth had had its divine effect upon them, and had brought them into a position where He could manifest Himself to them.

This is the great test for our hearts. If the truth affects us in a divine way, it must put us outside what is of man. And the truth is presented to us in a Person; it is not a mere collection of doctrines; it is presented in a Person, and that Person is the Son of God. If we are moved and affected by it—if we are attracted by its blessedness—we shall most surely be delivered from the influence of what obtains here, and we shall be led into conscious association with the Son of God. This is the great privilege of the assembly. To thus sever us in spirit and affection from the present order of things, and to lead us into conscious association with the Son of God, is the divine effect of the truth.

THE WAY OF HOLINESS

Hebrews 12: 1–14

Two things characterise the way of holiness. One is the attractiveness of Christ in glory, and of the purpose of God as set forth in Him, which puts us in the race and maintains us there, and the other is the chastening of the Lord, by which we are disciplined and free from things which are not according to God's holiness.

Difficulties are apt to discourage us if we do not see the true character of the race we are exhorted to run, and if we do not know the gracious use which God makes of the attendant exercises. The first thing we need is to be assured that we are in the right path, and then it is a great cheer to know that whatever opposition comes in the way is discipline for us, and is "for our profit, that we might be partakers of His holiness."

A man does not run very fast when he is not quite sure that he is in the right road. He is apt to be looking aside or behind, and every unexpected obstacle raises a doubt in his mind. The Hebrew believers had taken what was to them an entirely new road in becoming Christians; they were breaking away from religious associations of long standing and divine origin, and the only outward result was that they were plunged into difficulties and persecutions. Under such circumstances it became needful for God to encourage them by reminding them that the path of faith was no new thing. The eleventh chapter proved this. It is the history of men and women who trod a path in which were difficulties and dangers of every kind, and who in different ways *gave up the earth*. They accepted strangership, reproach, sufferings, and death in this world, because they looked for "a better country, that is, a heavenly." All this is brought out as encouragement; it is as much as to say, 'You see you are in the right road; now, *go on*.' When you are sure you are in the right road, the more difficulties there are in it the more anxious you are to shorten the journey, so you *run*. The Spirit of God calls upon us to 'run with endurance the race that is set before us.'

It has often been said that the first question with a soul is, Heaven or Hell? We can all understand John Bunyan's pilgrim running to the wicket gate with his fingers in his ears lest any voice should persuade him to turn back. It was heaven or hell with him; his eternal weal or woe was at stake. I dare say some of us ran rather fast at that stage of our experience. But further on in his journey, when the pilgrim came to the hill Difficulty and found the arbour, he settled down and went to sleep. The second question with the soul is, Heaven or Earth? Many are glad enough to escape hell who are not at all anxious to get away from earth. They settle down and go to sleep instead of running.

Of course no one would *run* to a place he did not want to reach, but if we are partakers of the heavenly calling, and know the heavenly Priest, our hearts are attracted to heaven; we have links with heaven, and heaven is an attractive place to us. I do not believe anyone is in the race here spoken of who does not like heaven better than earth. The Son of God has come down from heaven that He might throw the golden chain of divine love round our hearts and link us with Himself for ever. And He is now in heaven to attract our affections thitherward. Heaven is a most attractive place to everyone whose affections are set upon Christ, and such are all eager to run the race which has heaven for its goal. This race is not, as some suppose, the race of life; it is a moral journey—a race from earth to heaven—and those who are in it have turned their faces to heaven, and they want to get morally away from the earth and nearer to heaven.

The first indication that one has entered upon this race is the discovery that certain things are a hindrance to us; we begin to feel the "weights." Some believers do not seem to have any "weights"; you never see them laying anything aside. The fact is, they have never made a start in the race. A man who was sitting still might have a heavy weight in his pocket without being conscious of it, but if he began to run he would soon feel it and want to lay it aside. The longer and faster you run the more sensitive you become to "weights."

There is a close affinity between "weights" and "sin," but still there are things which we could hardly speak of as "sin" which may be serious "weights." For example, I could not say that to be on friendly terms with a half-hearted or worldly believer was exactly a *sin*, but it might become a heavy *weight* to anyone who really wanted to get on. So far as I have seen, companionship with undecided and half-hearted Christians is as spiritually injurious as friendship with unconverted people. "Go from the presence of a foolish man, when thou perceivest not in him the lips of knowledge." I have known many Christians who have discovered that a tobacco-pipe was a "weight," and I have not yet met a believer who felt that he had been helped heavenward by reading the newspaper. Worldly literature is a heavy "weight" to many. There is nothing in it to attract the heart to Christ in glory; it drags the mind and heart down to the earth. And, what was, perhaps, specially in the mind of the Spirit, an earthly system of religion is a great "weight." Judaism had all the sanction of a divine origin and the splendour of an imposing ritual; it was invested with a halo of traditional glory which acted powerfully on human feelings of veneration for antiquity. Yet, for the Christian, all this was a "weight" to be laid aside, a useless encumbrance, a positive hindrance. And we have the same hindrance to lay aside today, for Christianity has been perverted into a modified kind of Judaism, in which people are occupied with religious things on earth, and thus hindered from running the race to heaven. It would be a great gain if all Christians were exercised to keep their hearts free from the influence of religious things on earth.

At this point I may say that some believers make a mistake in fancying they are much hindered by things which are really a help to them. They complain of the opposition they meet with at home, and of the many trials they have in connection with their daily work, and so on, and they fancy they could get on much better if their circumstances were altered. But these things are not "weights" to be laid aside; they are part of God's helpful discipline, and it would be a spiritual loss to be without them. I have known Christians fret and chafe under their circumstances, and seek to change them, until God has given them their request, and the result has been leanness in their souls.

Then *sin* is to be laid aside. It is represented as a garment ever ready to entangle the feet. *Sin* is that which is contrary to the will of God, and if we allow it our feet are entangled and we cannot run. This is a very solemn and practical thing. There must be decision of heart to part company with that which is not according to the will of God. It is sometimes said that things will 'drop off,' and this is made the excuse for a good deal of self-indulgence. They have to be *laid aside*. Let me exhort my younger brethren to be uncompromising in this matter. You cannot afford to hesitate or parley when sin is in question.

Jacob's preparation for Bethel is a fine illustration of all this (Gen. 35: 1–4). There were "earrings" and "garments" which might have been all right in

Mesopotamia, but they would not do for Bethel. These things answer to the "weights." There were also found with them "strange gods"—things positively contrary to God—answering to "sin." And both earrings and idols had to be hidden "under the oak which was by Shechem" before Jacob and his family were ready for "the house of God."

Believers may go on a long time cherishing many fragments of worldliness, and often having in the background that which is known to be contrary to God. But there comes a moment in the history of the soul when the attractiveness of God's calling lays hold upon it, and it shakes itself free from its entanglements, and clears itself of its unholy links with the world, in order to enjoy its divine privileges. Shechem is the place of uncompromising decision. It is where Joshua said to the people, "choose you this day whom ye will serve... as for me and my house, we will serve the Lord." 'Now therefore put away the strange gods which are among you, and incline your heart unto the Lord God of Israel' (Joshua 24: 15, 23). It is at Shechem, morally speaking, that the soul sets itself and strips itself for the race. And the tree mentioned in Genesis 35: 4 and again in Joshua 24: 26 is very suggestive of the cross. The man who has been at Shechem, and has laid aside every weight and sin, can say, "God forbid that I should glory, save in the cross of our Lord Jesus Christ, whereby the world is crucified unto me, and I unto the world" (Gal. 6: 14). Beloved friends, have we reached this point? To what extend are we really set for Christ and heaven?

The motive power for all this lies in 'looking off unto Jesus.' If a Christian surrenders or lays aside anything without an adequate divine motive, he will either secretly hanker after it, and probably ere long return to it, or he will take credit to himself for having given it up, and will thus become self-righteous and spiritually proud. A certain school of religious teachers at the present day make much of 'surrender' as the way to attain blessing, but it ends in *self-sufficiency*, because the only motive that is presented for it is the acquisition of a better spiritual state, or power for service, or something of that kind. A *divine motive and attraction* is needed if souls are to be drawn into the race and prepared to surrender things in a truly spiritual way, and this divine motive and attraction is an Object outside ourselves altogether. It is CHRIST IN GLORY.

The Blessed One who is here presented to us as "the Author and Finisher of faith" could say, "I have set the Lord always before me" (Psalm 16: 8). He ever found His object and motive in God. He was here altogether *for God*—moving in absolute divine perfection over the whole course of faith, so that there is not a step in faith's pathway which His feet have not trodden—and this at all cost to Himself. For not only did He endure the "contradiction of sinners against Himself" all through His course, but He did actually resist "unto blood, striving against sin." Nothing could move Him from that path which,

"Uncheered by earthly smiles,
Led only to the cross."

He would give up His life, He would give up the earth, but He would not give up the will of God. His heart was glad and His glory rejoiced, even in prospect of being cut off and having nothing here. For "the path of life" lay through death, and "fulness of joy" and "pleasures for evermore" were set before Him in resurrection. He gave up the earth where Jehovah had nothing, and His heart was set on that bright and blessed scene where everything reflected the glory of God. In view of this He endured the cross and despised the shame, and He is now "set down at the right hand of the throne of God."

The "path of life" involves death here—it involves being *nothing* here. It is a very great thing to be so under the attraction of Christ and of the place where He is, that we are prepared to accept death here—prepared to become *nothing* here. Christ endured the cross and despised the shame because the vision of His soul was filled with the glories and joys of a brighter world, and it is as that world—and Himself, its blessed Centre—are before our hearts that we can accept the cross here. We can accept the "chastening of the Lord" which reduces and makes nothing of us, but which in doing so makes us partakers of God's holiness.

You may depend upon it that this is not an easy path for the flesh. Indeed, the word here translated "race" is generally rendered "conflict" or "fight." It is a path in which all kinds of opposition will be met. And let me say, for the sake of young believers, that it is always the next step which seems most difficult. The enemy concentrates all his power at the point where the Spirit of God is seeking to lead you on. Satan's great object is to discourage us so that we may turn aside and be hindered in our spiritual progress. He will put darkness and difficulty around the next step, whatever it is, but if you press on you will find that three-fourths of the difficulties will melt away as you advance, and the remaining fourth will be turned by the grace of God into helpful discipline for you. Then:

"Ye fearful saints, fresh courage take:
The clouds ye so much dread
Are big with mercies, and shall break
In blessings o'er your head."

And after all, the hindrances are nothing if compared with the blessed attraction of Christ in glory. Paul could say, "I count all things but loss, for the excellency of the knowledge of Christ Jesus my Lord: for whom I have suffered the loss of all things, and do count them but dung, that I may win Christ" (Phil. 3: 8). This is the language of one who was pressing on in the race, commanded by the object which he had in view, and rejoicing to have laid aside the weights that once hindered him.

Endurance is needed in this race, and this can only be imparted as the goal is kept in view. We may have often known what it was to be roused up by a stirring word, but incentives of this kind do not give power for *endurance*. They are like the crack of the whip, which makes the old horse mend his pace for a few yards, but he is soon back at his old jog-trot. What is needed for *endurance* is to have Christ commanding the heart. Turn the tired horse's head towards home, and see how he will go! We want more of the attraction of HOME—more of the attraction of that blessed Person who is the Centre of all thoughts of God, and of the place where He is. This will give *endurance* in the race, and nothing else will.

The joys and the exaltation which are of God—faith's pleasures and heritage—are connected with another scene. *Here* is the place of faith's conflicts and endurance. Hence there are difficulties, pressures, afflictions, persecutions, and innumerable trials which are peculiar to the path of faith. The man of faith will not anticipate an easy time in this world; he knows that he is going against the stream; he counts upon having to meet opposition and to suffer reproach; he freely accepts that the path on which he has entered involves the surrender of status here, and of the honours and pleasures which attach to life in this world. In short, he is treading a path which leads morally

FROM EARTH TO HEAVEN.

He esteems it a great honour from God that he is called in some measure to suffer in the path of faith, and he is greatly strengthened to face the difficulties and opposition by the consideration of the blessed fact that all faith's difficulties and conflicts are discipline for his profit.

In the path of faith we come into conflict with sin, and the pressure may be and often is very severe—men and circumstances may seem to be arrayed against us by satanic power; but we may be assured that God is above all and behind all that is happening, and faith would receive it all as "the chastening of the Lord"—a chastening needed "for our profit, that we might be partakers of His holiness." Every difficulty in the path of faith is discipline for us. It is not a weight to impede us; it is a belt to gird us so that we may run better.

It is evident that we can escape this kind of chastening if we choose to do so. It is only found in *the path of faith*, and unless we are in that path we shall not have it. It is written, that "if they had been mindful of that country from whence they came out, they might have had opportunity to have returned" (Heb. 11: 15). A worldly believer escapes the reproach of Christ; a carnal professor knows nothing of the difficulty of going against the stream; such cannot be said to be in conflict with sin, nor are they running the race of faith. I purpose to speak later on about other kinds of chastening which we may have, but for the present I speak of it as we find it presented in Hebrews 12, where the chastening is evidently in the form of

DIFFICULTIES ENCOUNTERED IN THE PATH OF FAITH.

But it may be helpful at this point to consider for a few moments the great end which God has in view in every form of chastening. It is "for our profit, that we might be partakers of His holiness"; and though "no chastening for the present seemeth to be joyous, but grievous: nevertheless, afterward it yieldeth the peaceable fruit of righteousness unto them which are exercised thereby" (Heb. 12: 10, 11).

I should like to point out what it is to be a partaker of God's holiness. I can only suggest the thought of it, and you may work it out for yourselves. It has often been said that Scripture gives the history of two men—Adam and Christ. And the whole history leads to the conclusion that *Adam* will not do for God, but CHRIST will. The summing up of the whole truth of Christianity is that there is only one Man before God for His pleasure, and that Man is CHRIST. The holiness of God necessitates the absolute setting aside of man in the flesh, but finds its eternal rest and satisfaction in CHRIST. We see the condemnation of sin in the flesh at the cross, and God is bent upon His children being made partakers of His holiness. There is a necessity for the practical displacement in us of that which was judged and removed from before God at the cross. Chastisement is always "for the destruction of the flesh." It always has the effect of reducing and bringing to nothing the activity and energy of man's will and natural powers. How His chastening exercises us to this end we may learn in three typical cases which present illustrations of the three kinds of chastening to which the children of God are subjected. The three cases I refer to are those of Paul, Job and David.

In 2 Corinthians 11: 23–28 we have a long list of sufferings which came upon Paul because of his being in the path of faith. And in the following chapter he speaks of "a thorn in the flesh, the messenger of Satan to buffet me, lest I should be exalted above measure," which was given to him because "the abundance of the revelations" might otherwise have lifted him up in spiritual pride. Paul's sufferings were the consequence of his devotedness and energy in the path of faith, or they were rendered necessary because of the exceptional favour which vouchsafed to him peculiar and blessed revelations. And I think we do not fail to see the result of the chastening in the spiritual history of the beloved apostle.

Paul must have been a man of great natural energy, and yet he was brought to glory in his weaknesses that the power of Christ might tabernacle over him. He had to learn that if "a man in Christ" could be caught up to the third heaven, it was a man 'IN CHRIST' who could go there. As a man in the flesh, he had to find himself still subject to the terrible buffetings of "a messenger of Satan." And the practical effect of the buffeting was that, as to himself, he was conscious of nothing but weakness. All the energy that belonged to him naturally was reduced. Do you think that any of us like this process? I am sure we do not. Nothing but the present "supply of the Spirit of Jesus Christ"—the present ministry to our hearts of the grace of Christ—will enable us to bear it. "My grace is sufficient for thee," said the Lord to His tried and devoted servant. The grace of the Lord is sufficient to make us willing to be weak and small. And when, by His grace, we are willing to be weak, we learn the blessed secret that "My strength is made perfect in weakness."

Discipline breaks down what is of the flesh, but when we are willing, through the grace of Christ, that it should be broken down, we find that instead of being *spiritually* weakened we have gained immensely. The knowledge of this enabled Paul to say, "Most gladly therefore will I rather glory in my infirmities, that the power of Christ may rest upon me. Therefore I take pleasure in infirmities, in reproaches, in necessities, in persecutions, in distresses for Christ's sake: for when I am weak, then am I strong." Thus, conscious of nothing but weakness in himself, he found all-sufficient grace and strength in Christ. Often when a caravan is crossing the desert some member of the company will fall sick, and will at last become so feeble that they are obliged to leave him behind to die. And in such cases they will often stretch a little tent over the dying man, to shield him from the fierce rays of the sun until he breathes his last. Some such figure was present to the apostle's mind when he said, 'Most gladly therefore will I rather glory in my weakness, that the power of Christ may *tabernacle over me*.' He says, in effect, 'I am just a mass of weakness, without a single pulsation of power in myself, but I accept this weakness with joy because it becomes the occasion for the power of Christ to tabernacle over me.' It is perfectly lovely. The strength and energy of Paul as a man in the flesh were displaced by the grace and strength of Christ. He thus became a partaker of God's holiness—the broken and reduced, but happy vessel of divine grace and power.

And we cannot read the epistle to the Philippians without seeing the gracious effect of a life of discipline in the school of God. The complete setting aside of his own will; the absorbing expectation and hope that CHRIST might be magnified in his body, whether by life or death; the lovely spiritual affections which shine out in so many ways; indeed, the whole epistle, so far as it presents the spirit and character of the writer, is one beautiful cluster of "the peaceable fruit of righteousness."

A second form of chastening comes to us in the way of

THINGS COMMON TO MEN,

of which we get a full illustration in the history of Job. I think Job had to endure every kind of suffering that is common to men. He had to taste the sorrow of bereavement, of the loss of property, and of terrible personal affliction. But God's end in it all was that Job might profit and become a partaker of His holiness. Job had a good deal of what we might call his own holiness before, but not until the end of the book do we find him really in the line of God's holiness. Like many others, he had connected the fruit of God's grace with himself, and in a certain way had taken credit to himself for that which divine grace had wrought in him. There had been much in him that was the fruit of grace, but it had turned into a kind of spiritual self-satisfaction.

In connection with Job's history we learn a principle of the greatest importance. That is, he never got the good of the chastening until he found himself in the presence of the Lord. It was when Paul turned to the Lord that he got the profit and benefit of his chastening, and I believe it is ever thus. It is in the presence of the Lord that we get the good of chastening. One has seen people go through great sorrow and suffering without getting much good from it, and I think in such cases there is no real turning to the Lord about it—no true recognition of His hand in it. Hence the Holy Ghost says, "despise not thou the chastening of the Lord, nor faint when thou art rebuked of Him: for whom the Lord loveth He chasteneth, and scourgeth every son whom He receiveth." It is of great importance that we should recognise the hand and heart of God in any chastening that comes upon us. This puts us, as it were, in His presence, to learn there the profitable lessons He would teach us.

Job, in the presence of God, says, "I abhor myself, and repent in dust and ashes." Now he has learned his lesson; he has discovered that man after the flesh is an object to be abhorred; he is now a partaker of God's holiness. And the peaceable fruit of righteousness comes out, in that he prays for his friends. He conducts himself toward them according to divine grace, in spite of all their hard speeches. He thus becomes to them the practical exponent of grace—a subject with which they were very little acquainted.

There is a third kind of chastening, which comes upon us in the form of

CORRECTION FOR SIN.

For an illustration of this, and of its effect, I should like you to consider the history of David. You have, no doubt, noticed that the Spirit of God has brought together, in 2 Samuel 22, 23, two of David's songs. One belongs to his early days, for he "spake unto the Lord the words of this song, in the day that the Lord had delivered him out of the hand of all his enemies, and out of the hand of Saul." The other contains "the last words of David." What a contrast there is between the two! In the first it is all triumph, he is exulting in what God has done for him; but in the last, as he thinks of the character of the one who is to rule over men in the fear of God, he has to say sorrowfully, "Although my house be not so with God." Forty years of discipline come between these two songs. How suggestive is this contrast!

Many of us have probably known what it was to rejoice in the grace of God without having apprehended very much of the true character of the flesh. It has often been noticed that where there is the greatest exuberance of joy in young converts, there is often a levity which fails to take into account that the flesh is unchanged. In such cases the grace of God is taken up in a self-confident way; there is very little self-distrust, or sense of weakness and dependence. And the inevitable consequence is a fall, or a succession of falls, that gradually bring home to the consciences of believers their utter weakness and incapacity as in the flesh.

We not only learn thus by our falls and back-slidings, but oftentimes these become the occasion of direct chastening on God's part, and we may have to suffer under God's government for years, or for a lifetime, the consequences of our sin and folly. David fell into a sin, the consequences of which he had to suffer all his life. He repented, and his sin was put away, but he had to suffer its governmental consequences all his life. "The sword shall never depart from thine house." But all this chastening—solemn as it was in itself, and sad as was the conduct which necessitated it—turned to David's profit, and in the lowly and chastened spirit of his "last words" we can see him a partaker of God's holiness. For if he has to say, "my house be not so with God," he has another Person in view, of whom he can say, "He shall be as the light of the morning, when the sun riseth, even a morning without clouds; as the tender grass springing out of the earth by clear shining after rain." He had learned to distrust everything connected with his own house; but he had also learned the preciousness and beauty of CHRIST, and the stability of God's purpose in Him, "Although my house be not so with God; yet He hath made with me an everlasting covenant, ordered in all things, and sure: for this is all my salvation, and all my desire." God's purposes secured in Christ were now not only all his *salvation*, but all his *desire*. Thus he became a partaker of God's holiness.

Then, again, when he numbered the people (2 Sam. 24), he was not thinking of God, but of David. It was to make much of David that he would have his people numbered, even though their moral condition was such that they were not willing to pay the half-shekel of redemption money, which was requisite to avert a plague (Ex. 30: 12). God would only have His people numbered on the ground of redemption, and it would appear from the result that the people were not in a moral condition to take this ground when David numbered them. As a consequence of the numbering of the people, a pestilence broke out amongst them, and seventy thousand people died. This was the terrible governmental consequence of David's sin and foolishness. It is true that the whole moral state of Israel was brought to light, and God's judgment came upon it, but the pride of David's heart was the thing that gave occasion to this solemn visitation.

Nor was the chastening lost upon him, for when he saw the angel that smote the people, he said, "Lo, I have sinned, and I have done wickedly: but these sheep, what have they done? Let thine hand, I pray thee, be against me, and against my father's house" (2 Sam. 24: 17). When in vainglorious pride he had said, 'number ye the people, *that I may know* the number of the people,' he was far from being a partaker of God's holiness. He was in a spirit of self-importance—in a state of sin. But when he said, "I have sinned, and I have done wickedly... Let thine hand, I pray thee, be against me," he recognised *himself* as nothing but a fit subject for divine judgment. He was then a partaker of God's holiness—morally delivered, as the effect of divine chastening, from the sinful self-importance which had led him astray. He had to confess, "Before I was afflicted I went astray; but now have I kept Thy word." (Psalm 119: 67). And he could also add, "It is good for me that I have been afflicted; that I might learn Thy statutes" (Psalm 119: 71).

But it is perfectly lovely to see how all the chastening which came upon David had its blessed "afterward." So that, though he had long years of affliction and sorrow, in which the governmental consequences of his sins came upon him in a terrible succession of calamities, yet, after all, his sun had a glorious setting. Instructed and humbled by all the chastening, he is found at the end of his days laying himself out for the building of the house of God (1 Chron. 22: 5, 14; 29: 2–5, 13–18).

There is something exquisitely beautiful in all this, if we look at it as the result of God's chastening. How entirely the sin that occasioned the chastening, and the sorrow that accompanied it, are eclipsed by the magnitude and preciousness of "the peaceable fruit of righteousness" which it yielded in due season! There is no more lovely picture in the Word of God than that of David in his last days—laying himself out for the house of God—rejoicing to give back to God everything that God had bestowed upon him; in short, expending himself and all his treasures for a work which was altogether for the glory of God, and of which another was to have the credit.

I trust we may be helped by what has been before us at this time to see the character and object and result of "the chastening of the Lord." It is a great thing for us to understand God's ways with us. I am sure there is great encouragement in the thought of divine chastening if we apprehend it aright. Hands often hang down, and knees are feeble, because we do not know the secret of God's ways with us. We get discouraged and depressed by things which are really most needful and profitable for us. If our hearts are set to run in the way of holiness, all the difficulties we encounter in the path of faith are the needed discipline to remove that which hinders our spiritual prosperity. And if we are passed through trials and sufferings such as are common to men, we must not suppose that they come to us by chance; too often such things are taken as a matter of course, the Lord's hand is not distinctly owned in them, and this is really despising the chastening of the Lord. Chastening does not profit us until we hear the voice of the Lord in it. Then, again, if we suffer, as many of us do in one way or another—chastening for sin and folly—let us not be discouraged and depressed by it, but rather let us rejoice that the love of God is set upon our being "partakers of His holiness." After all, nothing is destroyed or weakened by chastening but the flesh. Regarding ourselves as subjects of the work of God, we are in no wise hindered or impeded by God's chastening; on the contrary, we are immensely and divinely helped by it. We cannot derive profit, and God cannot derive pleasure, from what is of the flesh; and God's holy discipline reduces that which is altogether unprofitable, so that we may not be hindered from true "profit."

No greater end could be proposed to us, and none more attractive to a spiritual mind, than that we should be "partakers of his holiness." And every divine chastening has its "afterward," its blessed answer and recompense even here. I believe a moment comes in the history of every saint when he comes in view of "the end of the Lord," and in the estimation of his heart the end reached is well worth the painful course which has had to be travelled over to reach it. We may have to wander "in the wilderness in a solitary way," we may by the way, like those of old, be "hungry and thirsty," and our souls may faint in us, but when we reach the end which God has in view—"a city of habitation"—we see that the way by which He has led us is "the right way." It may be a "way" rendered necessary by our sin and folly, but it is, after all, a "right way," and we learn eternal lessons in it, the profit and blessing of which I believe God makes our hearts conscious of even here. In result we become partakers of God's holiness.

I knew a young servant of the Lord whose career of usefulness was suddenly cut short, as men would say, by an attack of chronic rheumatism which affected every joint in his body, and reduced him to perfect helplessness. After he had lain in bed, quite unable even to feed himself, for about ten years, I asked him one day what he thought of the Lord's dealings with him. A heavenly smile shone upon his face as he replied, 'I can do nothing but praise Him for it all.' I think he had come in view of "the end of the Lord." He had got the recompense even here.

This is a blessed result of chastening which nothing else could impart, an after-yielding of the peaceable fruit of righteousness, which is more than a recompense for the suffering which precedes it. The whole secret comes out when the beloved apostle says, "we which live are alway delivered unto death for Jesus' sake, that the life also of Jesus might be made manifest in our mortal flesh."

THE BRIGHT AND MORNING STAR

John 1: 29–39; **Matthew 25:** 1–10;
Revelation 22: 16, 17, 20

It would hardly be questioned, I suppose, that for a number of years there has been considerable interest amongst believers generally in truths connected with the Second Coming of the Lord. Nor could it be denied that those truths have been very widely accepted by the children of God. It is a very striking feature of God's ways with His saints that so much attention has been called to those truths during the present century. The significance of this has been often pointed out. There can be no doubt that the moment of the Lord's return draws nigh, and "it is high time to awake out of sleep." In view of this I desire to bring before you the Scriptures I have read, and I trust they may come to our hearts in freshness and power as a present ministry from the Lord.

I want to press the importance of *personal acquaintance with the One who is coming*. There cannot be much desire for His coming on the part of those who are not personally acquainted with Him. And I think the great mark of personal acquaintance is that we seek His company. I cannot believe there is much true desire for His coming in any heart that does not seek His company *now*.

The passage I read from John 1 shows us how two disciples became personally acquainted with Christ.

He was so presented to their hearts, and they were so attracted to Him that their one desire was to be in His company. Now, beloved brethren, I bring this before you because I am convinced that it is this alone which will make us "ready" in our affections for the return of the Bridegroom, and enable us to say "Come" in concert with "the Spirit and the bride." It is all very well to read books and hear addresses on the Second Coming of the Lord, and to search the Scriptures on the subject, but something more than this is needed to make us "ready" to meet Him.

I take for granted that I am addressing believers on the Lord Jesus Christ. You know that your sins are forgiven; you rejoice in the assurance that by the one offering of Christ you are "perfected for ever." As to any question of imputation of sin you are clear through your Saviour's blood. You are justified. We must begin with this. A purged conscience, and the Spirit as a divine link with Christ in glory, are needed before Christ can really be the object of the heart. He is presented to us here, first as the Lamb of God, then as the Baptiser with the Holy Ghost, and thirdly as the attractive and satisfying object of the hearts of His own.

God could not come out in the way of blessing to man until He had been glorified about sin. But the Lamb of God went into the place of sin that He might put it away by the sacrifice of Himself, and the first consequence of His death was that the "veil of the temple was rent in twain, from the top to the bottom." The way was open for God to come out in the fullest blessing, and in the glory of unmingled grace. God is a SAVIOUR-GOD. If there is one here who feels that death and judgment are his due, I can say to you that the Lamb of God has been under judgment and in death that He might remove every barrier that stood between your soul and the blessing of God. I can say to every repentant sinner—to every believer in Jesus—that not only is every barrier righteously removed, but the way in which they have been removed is the most wonderful and blessed testimony to *the love of God*. "God commendeth His love toward us, in that, while we were yet sinners, Christ died for us" (Rom. 5: 8).

And now the Lamb of God is seated in all the light and glory of the Father's throne. A shining track has been made from the depths of death and judgment to the heights of glory. We follow that shining track through the opened heavens to the right hand of God. We can go in. No device of hell can separate the redeemed from the Redeemer, or hinder Him from bringing the "many sons to glory." By His one offering we are perfected for ever; our consciences are purged; we have peace with God. Every believer in Jesus is before God in the infinite efficacy of the blood of the Lamb, and is in God's sight "whiter than snow."

Then, further, the Son of God as risen and glorified is the Baptiser with the Holy Ghost. By His death we are cleared of everything that attached to us as children of Adam, and now by the gift of the Spirit we have a link with Him in the place where He is. All that the grace of God has effected for us by the work of Christ was in view of our having a link with Him. It is inconceivable blessing. We are cleared *that we might have a link with the One who has cleared us*. Alas! it is to be feared that, with many, the Holy Ghost is grieved and hindered, and is not at liberty to make good this link with Christ in the hearts of believers. But where this is the case the believer reaps but little benefit from the Spirit. The normal action of the Spirit would be to form a link of affection between the believer and Christ such as that which subsisted between Jonathan and David (1 Sam. 18: 1–4). And this would naturally result in His becoming the object of our hearts, and His company the supreme desire of our souls.

The great gain of having the Spirit is that He makes the glory of Christ shine in the believer's heart, and this we see in figure in the two disciples who heard John speak. The glory of Christ shone into their hearts, and separated them from everything here. They were "*ready*" for His company, for He had thrown everything else into the shade, and made Himself supreme in their affections. They had previously been disciples of the greatest servant of God upon earth at the moment, but when the *Son of God* came into the vision of their hearts they left John. The glory of Christ eclipsed everything for them, and captivated their hearts. "One thing" they desired and sought after—His company. And this shows that they must have a sense of His love. They might not have been able to explain it, but His love had established itself in their hearts. It is *love* that desires the company of its object. The Father was drawing them to Christ by giving them a sense of the blessedness and love of Christ. And, beloved brethren, it is not otherwise today. Would that all our hearts had a sense of this. The Father is working by the Spirit to bring about the same result today. I trust many here know something experimentally of the reality of this; and if not, that we may be thoroughly awakened in heart, and exercised in conscience about our condition.

We are here as professed followers of Christ, and He challenges all our hearts at this moment with the searching question, 'WHAT SEEK YE?' Ah! *He knows* what we are after, but He challenges our hearts that we may be obliged, as it were, to declare ourselves. It is good sometimes to be obliged to give account of ourselves. Now are we prepared to be thus challenged? Are we so clear of the world, and so free from the tastes and motives of the flesh, that we can meet the challenge without confusion of face? Do our secret hours bear witness to the fact that we long after Himself? Or do they find us occupied with the ledger, the newspaper, with a thousand things that pertain to this life and to the world, so that—though we may sometimes sigh in the weariness of our way, and the Spirit of God may occasionally turn our souls heavenward with desire to breathe the atmosphere of divine love in the company of Christ—it cannot be said that we really "seek" His company at all?

The two whose course we are following were prepared for the challenge. Nay, it must have fallen on their ears as a most welcome sound, assuring and encouraging them. Such a challenge was just what their hearts desired. It gave them an opportunity to declare themselves, and to put themselves in touch with Him. Now, beloved, is it so with ourselves? Do our souls make us "like the chariots of Amminadib" [my willing people] to run after Him? He will cause those that love Him to "inherit substance," and He will "fill their treasures"; and He says, "those that seek Me early shall find Me." May it be ours to take advantage of His love, and to seek His company, so that, going after Him with purpose of heart, we may be able to answer His challenge in the spirit of the earnest inquiry, 'Master, where dwellest THOU?'

The great blessedness of the Lord's gracious response, "Come and see," has often, I am sure, been food for our hearts. They are wonderful words if we consider all that is implied in them. It is the place "where He dwelt" that they were invited to "come and see." I suppose the youngest babe in Christ would instinctively understand that the Spirit of God intended to convey in these words something far deeper than the thought of a material dwelling-place. The glory that attracted the hearts of the two disciples to that Blessed One was a *moral* glory—a glory of divine perfections and love which only anointed eyes could discern or appreciate—and the place "where He dwelt" speaks to our hearts of a moral dwelling-place suited to Himself. In a word, the two disciples wanted to know Him *in His own circle*, and His love conferred upon them the freedom of that circle.

I should like to bring another Scripture into your minds in connection with this subject: John 20: 11–20. Here we find another captivated heart—another follower—another seeker. What were the best things of the earth to Mary's heart? Religion was keeping its "high day" in Jerusalem, but not for her. The excitement of the political circle was engrossing thousands, but its burning questions had no place in her heart. No doubt the cares of this life were known by her as by any of us, but they reigned not in her spirit. She had but one *grief*, as the disciples in chapter 1 had but one *Object*. His *presence* created a new world for their hearts, and His *absence* desolated the old world for Mary's heart. It cannot be said that she was strong in *faith* or *hope*, but she stands conspicuous for LOVE to His blessed Person. 'They have taken away MY LORD.' It may be she had little thought of where He dwelt, but it was the same affection which led the two disciples to ask, "Master, where dwellest Thou?" that prompted her to say, "Sir, if thou have borne Him hence, tell me where thou hast laid Him, and I will take Him away." And the same voice that had said, "Come and see," opened up to her a new world of everlasting love, and brought her consciously into a new association with Himself outside all the desolation of this scene of death, as by the one word "Mary" He called her into the presence of His unchanged and living love.

He revealed Himself to Mary, as He had in figure to the two disciples, *in His own circle*, and He made her the bearer of the wondrous message which was, we might say, the complete unfolding of all that was involved in the words, "Come and see." He was no longer to be touched and known in the old associations "after the flesh," but by the Spirit He might be touched in His new place as ascended to the Father. He takes a new place, but He will have His brethren in the most complete association with Himself in that new place. "I ascend unto My Father, and your Father; and to My God, and your God." In this way He invites us to "come and see" His dwelling-place, and to share it with Him.

But let none of us think lightly of this wondrous privilege, for He could only secure it for us by *His death*. As in the flesh we could never be in association with Christ, and if He had not died this holy privilege could never have been ours. Blessed be His name, He has removed in death, to the glory of God, all that we were as children of Adam. His death has ended our history before God as in the flesh, and divested us in the presence of infinite love of every trace of unsuitability to that love. How could we be free in His company if we did not know this? How could He claim us as His brethren on any other ground? Well may we adore Him for the triumphs of His love.

"In the triumph and the glory
Of Thy rest in love divine
Thou dost tell the wondrous story
How God's counsels made us Thine;

"How by dying Thou hast freed us
From the man of sin and shame,
That, unhindered, Thou might'st lead us
Now to know Thy Father's name."

It is as we enter into this that our hearts are drawn to Him, and we find ourselves in spirit outside everything that is of the world and of the flesh. And until we know something of the reality of this we cannot be said to be in heart "ready" for His return.

The effect of Mary's message was to gather the

disciples together outside everything that was of man. They were outside everything because of what Christ was to their hearts. Their hearts were illuminated by His love. With the doors shut to exclude the religious man after the flesh, they got the company of Christ and were glad. The world was only to them the scene of His rejection and death. And thus they were fitted to be sent by Him into the world in His interests. This was the beginning of Christianity. Can you imagine what the church would have been if she had maintained her first love? A company of hearts espoused to Christ, and satisfied with His company and love, and walking in strangership and rejection here in loyalty to Him. Surely if we got a true thought of it we should be ready to weep over the condition of the church today.

I now pass on to the second Scripture which we read at the beginning (Matt. 25). This Scripture is of great importance because it brings together in one view (1) the first love of the church, (2) the decline of that love, and (3) the awakening and revival thereof so as to make the wise virgins "ready" for the return of the Bridegroom.

1. The virgins "took their lamps, and went forth to meet the bridegroom." I do not intend to occupy you at this time with the foolish virgins, who set forth the lamentable condition of those who have the profession of Christianity without the reality of its blessings. The wise virgins represent the company of true saints who have "oil in their vessels"; that is, they have received the Spirit. All such at the beginning went forth to meet the Bridegroom. Their hearts were engaged with Himself, and they left every earthly association to have the joy of His company. This was what marked them—they sought His company. This is the great characteristic of first love.

2. "While the bridegroom tarried, they all slumbered

and slept." Here we see in picture the state of things which rapidly succeeded the pentecostal brightness. How soon had the Lord to say, 'Nevertheless I have against thee, that thou hast left thy first love' (Rev. 2: 4). He had lost His place in their hearts, and if that is the case the Christian slumbers and sleeps. It may sound like a paradox, but I have no doubt there may be works, and labour, and endurance, and much fidelity in respect of many things, while the heart slumbers and sleeps. (See Rev. 2: 2–5.) What is the value of Scripture knowledge, or of correct views on prophecy and ecclesiastical principles, if our *hearts* are sound asleep? You may ask, What is it to slumber and sleep? Well, I think it is to lose the consciousness of our association with Christ, so that the believer settles down into things here. If our hearts lose the consciousness of our association with Christ we are sure to become earthly-minded. And this is what has happened to the church. "All seek their own, not the things which are Jesus Christ's," says Paul to the Philippians; and again, 'For many walk, of whom I have told you often, even weeping… who mind earthly things.' It is this which has brought the church into the state of spiritual weakness and ruin in which it is found today. The virgins have "slumbered and slept."

3. "And at midnight there was a cry made, Behold the bridegroom cometh; go ye out to meet him." Here we see the intervention of God to bring about the result that there should be a company "ready" to meet the Bridegroom. And I think none would deny that there has been a very remarkable intervention of God in the actual history of the church. Every one of us here has benefited by that intervention, and some, it may be, to a very great degree. We have only to go back some four hundred years to find the almost universal sway of priestcraft and superstition in the Church. No doubt God maintained His elect all

through, but so far as any public light or testimony was concerned there was a long period of appalling and almost unbroken darkness. The Reformation was a loud cry which echoed far and wide amid the darkness, and it was followed by other movements which, though not attracting the same amount of public attention, produced probably a far deeper spiritual result amongst many who had been delivered as a consequence of the first movement from the thraldom of Rome. The present century has witnessed the recovery of much precious truth unknown in the Church since apostolic days; and within the last few years the Person of Christ, and the blessedness of the saints' association with Him in new creation, have been presented in a remarkable way to the hearts of believers. It is impossible to doubt that in this way the awakening cry, "Behold the bridegroom," has gone forth in a very distinct manner. Nor has it been without effect. Many have left the religious associations and human systems in which they were found. There has been, to some extent at any rate, a going out and a trimming of lamps.

I believe it is of immense importance for us to recognise the true nature of the present testimony of the Holy Ghost. It is the presentation of Christ Himself to the hearts of His own—'BEHOLD THE BRIDEGROOM.' We have often heard that the point of departure is the point of recovery. The point of departure in the church was when CHRIST lost His supreme place in the hearts of His own, and there is no recovery until He regains it. Some have thought that the cry, "Behold the bridegroom," was figurative of the revival of prophetic truth. No doubt God has graciously given much light on prophecy during the present century, but it has been only the necessary accompaniment of truths "concerning Christ and the Church." I do not believe the Spirit of God would occupy us with a series of prophetic facts; His mission is to present a PERSON. And I cannot help warning my younger brethren against much literature that is abroad on prophetic subjects. Books and pamphlets which occupy you with events and dates, and especially those which connect events occurring at the present time with prophecy, are to be shunned. The effect of them is to occupy souls very much with what is going on in the world, and I am sure the Spirit of God is not seeking to do this. He would present to our hearts the One who is in glory, and separate us even now to His company outside everything that is going on here.

"Then all those virgins arose, and trimmed their lamps." Here we see the effect of the midnight cry. The presentation of the Person who is coming immediately awakens exercise. It raises the question in the soul, 'Am I suitable to Him?' If there is no exercise of this kind, it is a sure indication that the soul is asleep. The exercise of every awakened heart leads to the discovery that the lamp need trimming—that there is that which needs to be judged and removed, so that we may be in conscious suitability to the One who is coming. When our hearts are illuminated by His love we are in conscious suitability to Him. It is not here a question of being perfected for ever by His one offering, of being cleansed by His blood, but of conscious suitability to Him by the Spirit. Many a believer who has no doubt as to the efficacy of His work is far from being in conscious suitability to Him, and where this is the case the lamp needs trimming. We do not reach this suitability without exercise, and may God enable each one of us to trim our lamps.

There are three steps by which the Spirit would lead us, if unhindered into conscious suitability to Christ.

1. "I am crucified with Christ: nevertheless I live; yet not I, but Christ liveth in me: and the life which I now

live in the flesh, I live by the faith of the Son of God, who loved me, and gave Himself for me" (Gal. 2: 20). Paul was conscious of a love which had divested him at its own cost of everything that was unsuited to itself. All that he was as a child of Adam had gone in the death of Christ from before God's eye, and he was so in accord with this—he had so reached it experimentally—that he could say, "I am crucified with Christ." He recognised nothing as life to God but CHRIST living in him; and the One who had thus set him free in the presence of divine love from all that attached to him as a man in the flesh was now the object of his heart. If you are saying, 'Oh that I could be in suitability to Christ! but I cannot improve my wretched self, and I cannot get rid of it,' I should like you to consider the infinite love that is here brought before us. The Son of God has undertaken in love to remove all my unsuitability, and to accomplish this He has given Himself. He has gone into death that He might free me from myself, and have me for Himself. And by His death I am entitled to be with God and with His Son as one set free from all that attached to me as a child of Adam. I think we could not help being drawn to the Lord if we realised this. As another has said, 'He has cleared the ground that He might occupy it.' It is a wonderful moment in the soul's history when it gets the consciousness of being *loved by the Son of God*. It is a most blessed thing to know Him in His greatness and glory, and to know that there is an eternal link of love between Him and me—love which has removed for its own satisfaction and at its own cost everything that I am morally as of the race of Adam, so that I might be free in the presence of that love. The Holy Ghost would illuminate our hearts with the light of this love. And with the light and warmth of this love pervading our hearts, the dim and worthless, though often cherished idols of the earth, would retire into the shade to which they properly belong, and heaven would become supremely attractive because of the One who is there. We have not merely deliverance, but the personal love of a DELIVERER.

2. "For both He that sanctifieth and they who are sanctified, are all of one: for which cause He is not ashamed to call them brethren" (Heb. 2: 11). Here we see a further unfolding of what His love has effected. It is not only that all our unsuitability as belonging to Adam's race has been removed in His death, but we are now in association with the One who has removed it. We are of Him; we derive from Him; we are "all of one" with Him. This is not the flesh sanctified; it is not Christ made "all of one" with our flesh, as modern theology so falsely teaches; it is not our flesh made "all of one" with Him; it is a new creation in which we are altogether apart from the flesh, associated in life and relationship with Christ risen, so that His Father is our Father, and His God our God. He is not ashamed to call us brethren, because in this new creation order there is no disparity between Himself and those whom He has sanctified. We are "all of one" with Him. The Holy Ghost would light up our hearts with the glory and love of this wondrous association with Christ.

3. "If I wash thee not, thou hast no part with Me" (John 13: 8). Such is the love of Christ that He cannot be satisfied without our company. It is to secure this that His priesthood is exercised to lift us above every pressure here, that we may join Him in the sanctuary. For this He washes our feet to free us from the influences of this present scene, so that we may have part with Him. To this end He is presented to our hearts by the Holy Ghost in the Scriptures, and in all true ministry, that our hearts may be drawn away from the earth where He is not to the scene of His exaltation and glory. He wants our company. His love delights to share with us the joys of that

blessed world where He has gone, and to make us familiar with the Father's presence—in a word, to have us near Himself.

Now, beloved brethren, is the light of all this love shining brightly in our hearts? I know that these precious things are true *for* all believers, but they are not made good *to* us until we appropriate them. They are things which have to be experimentally reached through exercise of soul. Every bit of Canaan from Dan to Beer-sheba belonged to the children of Israel by divine gift; but they had to take possession, and they did not *possess* any more than what their feet trod upon. Many of us are familiar with these Scriptures, but I put it first to myself and then to everyone here, Is *the love of Christ* the present illumination and joy of your heart? *If not, the lamp needs trimming*. It is the blessed work of the Holy Ghost to maintain the light of Christ's love in our hearts—He would feed that flame of love in our souls—but this will not be the case if we are wrapped in the slumber of earthly-mindedness. Nor will it be realised apart from exercise on our part. It is of necessity that the lamp should be trimmed. I venture to say that with each one of us there are things which are a hindrance to the Spirit of God; but if our hearts are truly awakened it will be our joy to disallow and set aside everything that obstructs and grieves that Holy One. It may be with some of us there are links with the world that have never been broken. Many believers are like two men who got into a boat to row across a river one very dark night. They pulled away some time without reaching the opposite side, and eventually discovered that they had forgotten to loosen the rope that fastened the boat to the bank of the river. Beloved brethren, have we no links that need to be severed, links with the world that hinder our spiritual progress, and grieve the Holy Ghost, and cause the light of divine love to burn dim in our hearts? 'Awake, thou that sleepest, and arise from among the dead, and Christ shall shine upon thee.'

It may cost us something to trim our lamps, but who can measure the gain? A single eye will inevitably lead to a trimmed lamp. That is, the heart in which Christ is supreme is sure to be diligent in the judgment and renunciation of what is not Christ. Then the lamp will be trimmed, and the whole body be "full of light." This is first love. Christ is everything, and the soul is in conscious suitability to Him. The awakened virgins with trimmed lamps got back to the point of departure. Then they were "ready" for the return of the Bridegroom.

Enoch in his day was "ready." It is not at all surprising that God translated him. He had walked apart from the earth's din and noise in moral suitability to God for three hundred years, and his translation was, if one might so say, the appropriate termination of such a course. Translation was not a great moral change for him. His circumstances were changed in a very wonderful way, I admit, but morally he had been "with God" for centuries. He was in moral suitability for translation. He was "ready." I do not think his departure created a gap in the political or social circles of the day. He had been outside all that for hundreds of years.

Elijah, too, had been apart from the idolatrous nation before he was translated. He was taking no part in the course of things around him. He was morally "ready" to go out of the world altogether. God grant that in this sense *we* may be "ready" for the return of the Bridegroom. I believe the special ministry of the Lord at the present time is to bring about this result, and all the activities of the Holy Ghost are to this end. God grant that we may know how to profit by it all—CHRIST becoming so really our treasure that our hearts may be *with Him*; and in result that our loins may be girded about, and our lights burning, and we ourselves like unto men that wait for their Lord.

I turn now, for a few moments, to Revelation 22: 16, 17, 20. There is something inexpressibly sweet and precious—something which lays hold of the heart with singular power—in this last presentation of the Lord Jesus to the hearts of His own. Such a comprehensive view of His blessed Person in varied characters—such a combination of suggestive titles—is rarely to be found in such brief compass.

First the sweet personal Name by which He made Himself known to us in our deep need as sinners—the sacred and saving Name—"I JESUS." In thus presenting Himself to our hearts does He not recall the untold grace in which He stooped so low that He might bring divine love into contact with all our sin and woe? Bethlehem, Nazareth, the shores of Galilee, come afresh before our hearts as we think of that Name, and the wondrous story of Calvary is woven into its precious syllables. "I JESUS." How it carries us back to the moment when our leprous souls first felt His cleansing touch—when first His hand of tenderness and might was laid upon our restless and fevered spirits—when first the healing virtue flowed forth from Him, responsive to faith's feeble touch—when first the music of His voice filled our hearts with gladness as we heard Him say, 'Thy sins are forgiven. Go in peace,' and a great calm overspread our consciences, storm-tossed with doubt and fear.

But this book reveals Him in other scenes—His eyes as a flame of fire; His voice as the sound of many waters; the glory-throne His rightful seat; the many crowns upon His brow; the Kingly Name on vesture and on thigh; yet still to His own He speaks as "I Jesus." For them He still wears—and delights to wear—His Name of saving love. What could appeal more sweetly to our hearts?

"I Jesus have sent Mine angel to testify unto you these things in the churches." Here we see Him as the Prophet making known the mind and ways of God, not indeed in the intimacy of affection, as when He declares the Father's Name to His brethren, but in that administrative way in which He makes known the truth of God from time to time as it is needed in the assemblies of His saints. For this there is a medium of communication—'I... have sent *Mine angel*.' It cannot be doubted that the Lord still acts in a way similar to this. He sends a ministry by some chosen vessel or vessels suited to the condition of His saints and to the present ways of God in the actual history of the church. Who can doubt that there was such a special ministry in the days of Luther and J.N.D., not to mention others less distinctly known? Truth from God suited to His present ways was declared in the days of these men "in the assemblies." Of course no new revelation was communicated, but special prominence was given to the truth needed at the time. We may look for and count upon this to the end. May we ever have an ear to hear the present testimony of the Lord in the assemblies.

"I am the root and the offspring of David." Jehovah's choice, and promises in sovereign grace, made David great. All that David was in a divine sense he derived from Jehovah—it was to Jehovah that he owed all the glory and power of his kingdom. Jehovah was the source of all those promises of kingly glory which, throughout the Word of God, connect themselves with David and his seed. It is this that I understand to be conveyed in the expression, "I am the root... of David." All that pertained to Jehovah is thus assumed in the most distinct way by Jesus. The Deity of the Messiah—so plainly asserted in Hebrews 1—thus shines fully and clearly forth.

As the *Root* of David He bestowed the promises, but as David's *Offspring* He will inherit them all in manhood. He is coming soon to bring all the glory in—to bind Messiah's honours upon His brow and reign before His ancients gloriously—to present in His own person, and to secure by His power, all that is promised in the prophecies of the Old Testament. In coming into manhood He inherited the titles and honours of the Messiah, and He will yet manifestly assume and display them. "The Lord God shall give unto Him the throne of His father David: and He shall reign over the house of Jacob for ever; and of His kingdom there shall be no end" (Luke 1: 32, 33).

"I Jesus" carries our hearts back to the day of His humiliation, and fills them with thoughts of the love which stooped so low to win and secure us for Himself. "The offspring of David" makes our hearts glow with anticipation of that coming day of glory which will soon shed its brightness from pole to pole, and from the river to the ends of the earth. But what have we in the interval between the day of His humiliation and the day of His supremacy? While the dark night of His rejection casts its shade on everything here, while the church mourns her absent Bridegroom, while men claim His inheritance as their own, and while declension and apostasy are written large upon that which bears His name, what is faith's resource and joy? It is HIMSELF, who, hidden from the eyes of a sleeping world, shines upon our hearts in heavenly lustre and beauty as 'the BRIGHT AND MORNING STAR.'

Then "let us not sleep, as do others," for the waking and watchful eye alone is refreshed by the Star in the sky. If we miss the blessed opportunity, which is ours now, of knowing our Saviour and Lord in this character, we shall never have it again. In the day of glory He will be known in other characters, but as the Bright and Morning Star He can only be known during the *night* of His rejection. Many peculiar privileges belong to those who are called by infinite grace to know Him in the time of His rejection, and not the least of these privileges is the blessed intimacy of a personal knowledge of Himself as the Bright and Morning Star. The empty glory of the world, and the self-aggrandisement and self-complacency of an unfaithful church become grief and sorrow to a heart that thus knows the Lord. For such a heart the shadow of His rejection rests on everything *here*, while every ray that shines from that Star is bright with divine love that attracts to its own circle everyone who truly knows it. If I have lost the world and its things, what have I gained? *I have a Person, and the love of that Person for my heart*. And when I think WHO that Person is, and how He has brought divine love to me, and how He draws my heart to Himself in an ineffable scene of divine affections, I begin to taste divine satisfaction.

Then I can say, "Come." The soul must be satisfied before it can say, "Come." I say, "Come," because I know the blessedness of the Person, and of all that He will bring. I am so enjoying it all in my heart—so living in it in the knowledge of Himself—that I cannot help saying, "Come." It is the spontaneous expression of a satisfied heart that feels the immeasurable need and loss of the scene where He is not, the expression, too, of bridal affection which desires to see Him honoured and supreme in the place where He died.

The effect of really knowing Him as the Bright and Morning Star is that, in concert with the Spirit and the bride, we say, "Come." Our lamps are trimmed: we are "*ready*." We are *in spiritual suitability* to the One who is coming. May it be so with us.